KEEPING WATCH

Reflections on American Culture, Education, and Politics

By

Paul F. Cummins

ISBN: 0-7596-6722-5

This book is printed on acid free paper.

1stBooks - rev. 04/18/02

The sun shines and carries away the shadowy remains of night. Horse-drawn carriages pick up the garbage, door to door. In the air the spider spins its threads of saliva. El Tornillo walks the streets of Melo. People in town think he's crazy. He carries a mirror in his hand and he looks at himself with furrowed brow. He doesn't take his eyes off the mirror.

"What are you doing, Tornillo?"

"I'm here," he says, "keeping watch on the enemy."

–*Eduardo Galeano*

DEDICATION

These essays are dedicated to the memory of my father, Paul S. Cummins (November 10, 1907 – March 25, 1983) and to my mother, Ruth Wenter, who recently (April 24, 2001) celebrated her 90th birthday.

ACKNOWLEDGEMENTS

I want to thank several people for their support in putting this book together. As always, my assistant, Adrienne McCandless, for typing, organizing, and monitoring all of these articles, and for her patience and ability to juggle many balls at the same time. A special thank you also to Alva Libuser for intelligently and critically reading, correcting, and making editorial comments on the enclosed articles. In addition, my appreciation of Nadia Lawrence for her thoughtful suggestions, fine tuning and editing of my final draft and a thank you to Jacqueline Stehr for her assistance. Also, I want to thank Robert Scheer for his writing; he is for me the model of a superb journalist. And finally, my appreciation to Peggy Clifford, Editor, and Michael Rosenthal, Publisher, of the *Santa Monica Mirror* for permission to reprint these articles.

OTHER BOOKS BY PAUL F. CUMMINS

Richard Wilbur

Dachau Song: The Twentieth-Century Odyssey of Herbert Zipper

For Mortal Stakes: Solutions for Schools and Society

TABLE OF CONTENTS

I) **CULTURE**

II) **EDUCATION**

CULTURE

EDUARDO GALEANO: KEEPING WATCH ON THE ENEMY

In virtually every corner of the globe, human beings are imprisoning, torturing, and killing others–usually for the simple fact that they are different from the power structure. Simultaneously, humans are destroying the beautiful varieties of plant and animal life. In addition, the relentless forces of materialistic-technological globalization have already led to the destruction of many indigenous cultures and threaten the remaining ones with extinction. And each time a people with different customs (that is, different from mainstream westernized-cocacolaized-disneyfied cultures) with different music, art, and language is erased from the planet, erased forever, then we are all lessened just a little bit more. Homogenization diminishes us all. It is a sad and depressing spectacle.

Nevertheless, sadness and despair are not only inadequate responses; they are themselves dangerous. We know that we are locked in a life and death struggle of limited consciousness vs. expanding consciousness. As an educator, I try to warn teachers against teaching hopelessness to the young, and I try to convince them that we all, especially teachers, need teachers ourselves.

Eduardo Galeano is one of the great teachers of this planet. His dazzling journey through old and new world cultures, his poetry, his fables and stories, his blend of human frailty–political fierceness–and mysticism... transport us into a world utterly unique. There is simply no one quite like him. For Galeano is one of the world's most fierce warriors, battling to preserve indigenous cultures. His weapon is his pen. Listen to his own words:

The flowering of cultural freedom, the freedom of diversity, is a feat ever more difficult for poor people and weak countries to achieve, condemned as they are to imitating the lifestyle imposed everywhere nowadays as the only possible way of life. With national industries having disappeared, plans for autonomous development forgotten, the state dismantled, symbols of sovereignty abolished, the countries that make up the vast shantytowns of the world have few opportunities to affirm their right to be themselves and proud of it. The right to be, the pride of being, collides with the function of servitude assigned to them by the international division of labor. Just as it contradicts the role of passive spectators in which they have been cast by the cultural industry and the mass media.

Today, culture is largely reduced to entertainment: The cultural industry should really be called the entertainment industry. Exaggerated though it may sound, I'm convinced the mercantile despotism of the mass-media entertainment industry is inflicting cultural damage on the world at least as devastating as the ethnic cleansing of Kosovo... Technological diversity is said to be democratic diversity. Indeed, nowadays technology places images, words and music within the reach of all, as never before in the history of humanity. But such good fortune becomes a dirty trick when private monopolies end up imposing a one-image, one-word, one-tune dictatorship on the planet. Even taking into account the exceptions–and fortunately there are exceptions, and not so few–this giant machinery tends to offer us thousands of ways of choosing between the same and the same. Are we all doomed to die of hunger or of boredom?

In the beginning of The Book Of Embraces, Galeano reminds us that the word in Spanish, *recordar*, `to remember' has its roots in the Latin *re-cordis*– which means "to pass back through the heart." Galeano's epic Memory Of Fire takes us back into the histories of the Americas through the heart of many cultures where he shows us what is worthy of celebration, as well as how humans can shrivel up their hearts.

In Walking Words, he presents us with the image of a man walking about with a mirror pressed to his face– "What are you doing" he is asked? He replies, "I'm keeping watch on the enemy." Yet, in spite of knowing full well who the enemies are, Galeano not only holds our faces to the mirror, he leads us into the domain of faith.

To read from The Book Of Embraces:

Yes, indeed: however hurt and shattered one might be, one can always find contemporaries anywhere in time, and compatriots anywhere in space. And wherever this happens, and for as long as it lasts, one is lucky to feel one is something in the infinite loneliness of the universe: something more than a ridiculous speck of dust, more than just a fleeting moment.

Eduardo Galeano is one of our contemporary compatriots and clearly his life and work is something much more than just a fleeting moment.

[Note: Eduardo Galeano received the Lannan Cultural Freedom Award in 1999.]

THE AWFUL RESPONSIBILITY OF TIME

The millennium prompted a spate of lists–the 50 most important *this*, the 100 most important *thats*, of the century.

In December 1999, the <u>Los Angeles Times</u> joined the listing frenzy by asking a number of writers to present neglected classics of the century. I've always been a bit of a list maker myself–perhaps it's a Ben Franklin gene from somewhere in my past–so I think I'll suggest and annotate a few of what I believe to be neglected 20th century masterpieces. In no particular order, here are five neglected classics I recommend.

One, <u>The Abolition of Man</u> by C.S. Lewis. Lewis is known to many for his children's classic–<u>The Chronicles of Narnia</u> –and to others for his Christian apologetics, i.e., <u>Mere Christianity</u> and <u>The Screwtape Letters</u>. His incisive and logically completing study, <u>The Abolition of Man,</u> is a superb argument against the 20th century infatuation with moral relativism. When you consider that Lewis wrote the book in 1947, before, for example, the possibility of genetic engineering, his arguments against considering human beings as "infinitely malleable" become not only relevant, but prescient. Lewis believes there are moral absolutes and that the function of education is to inculcate "just sentiments." He quotes Aristotle: "The aim of education is to make the pupil like and dislike what he ought." "Ought" is the key word. To Lewis there are absolute truths–he calls them the "tao," the reality beyond all predicates. These truths, values, moral laws (i.e., "thou shalt not commit murder") are not subject to debate; they are the yardsticks by which we measure behavior. Like this or not, Lewis' classic remains, at least for me, a critical book to ponder.

My second neglected classic would be <u>House Made of Dawn</u>, a novel (1969) by N. Scott Momaday. It is a haunting story of a young Native American who has just returned from World War II and finds himself caught between two worlds–the world of the white man's civilization which holds for him very little hope and much temptation to descend into drugs, dissipation, and self-loathing, and the other pull, the world of his forefathers, almost obliterated by the white man but nevertheless compelling if he can only learn to listen to the voices in the silence of the land. Leslie Marmon Silko's <u>Ceremony,</u> along with Momaday's <u>House Made of Dawn</u> are, I believe, two of the greatest Native American novels written.

My third nominee is a wonderful study of Modern (1870-1945) American reform by Eric Goldman entitled <u>Rendezvous With Destiny</u>. Goldman begins his discussions of an America in the 1870s "in which both the hopelessly poor and the overwhelmingly rich were limited in numbers," and the chief evil of the day he explains as "the alliance between industrialists." Writing this article in 2000, I cannot help but think that 130 years of reform efforts–while achieving some gains–have not fundamentally changed the distinctions between the rich and the poor, except that, unlike the 1870s, there are now *very many* hopelessly poor and *many more* obscenely rich.

The Age of Reform took on many issues, and Goldman brilliantly presents the clash of ideas. For example, consider the following antinomies:

> *No government interference with the industry of the people vs. government reform of corrupt practices and unholy alliances; the steady combination of businesses and formation of monopolies and huge trusts vs. small entrepreneurs and anti-trust advocates; intervention to assist corporations and big business vs. government intervention to assist men of little or no capital; those who interpreted the Constitution as a sacred text vs. those who viewed it as a human document written by propertied men.*

During this period of rapid industrialization with its concomitant growth of financial fortunes and economic and social stratification came a host of new problems: a new sneering condescension toward immigrants and ethnic groups (pejorative new words coined included "dago," "wop," and "kike,"); the growing difficulties of farmers and the decline of prestige in farming itself; the appearance of high mortgage rates, long work hours, and low wages; the shocking conditions in child labor; big city political machines reeking of patronage and corruption. All of these, and more, were issues Goldman outlines and which are certainly relevant today. If liberalism is ever to recover its vibrancy in American life, Goldman's book is a good place to remind ourselves of what liberalism at its best can be.

My fourth choice for this brief article is a book by Milovan Djilas entitled The New Class which had a profound impact on many people when it was published in 1965. Djilas was a Yugoslav Montenegro radical communist in the 1930s, imprisoned and tortured several times, a partisan in World War II fighting Nazis and Royalists along with Joseph Broz (alias Marshall Tito), and finally, the Vice President of Yugoslavia after the war. He was a true communist who believed in putting the theory into practice. When he expressed his beliefs that the new totalitarianism of Russia and Yugoslavia had simply created a new class of rulers replacing the old, aristocratic rulers, he was expelled from the party, lost his vice presidency, and was ultimately jailed–spending several years at hard labor as the price of his honesty. Like Orwell's *ANIMAL FARM*, Djilas' classic analysis of communism in *THE NEW CLASS* exposes the corruptive influence of power. Djilas died on April 20, 1995. *THE NEW CLASS* remains as a powerful testament to the human dream and right of freedom.

My final choice is Robert Penn Warren's <u>All The Kings Men</u> which is, I believe, the best political novel ever written in America. I have read and taught the book several times and, with each new reading, I see new applications, stylistic nuances, and connections within the book. It is masterfully crafted and is not–as some dismiss it–simply a fictionalized biography of Huey Long, the Kingfish of Louisiana in the '30s. No, <u>All The Kings Men</u> is a study of power, the relationship of ends and means, the nature of sin, and the possibilities of redemption. The language is rich, almost baroque, and the book is replete with humor, tragedy, history, suspense, and adventure. At the end of his journey, the narrator of the novel, Jack Burden, writes: "Soon now we shall go out of the house and go into the convulsion of the world, out of history into history and the awful responsibility of time."

Paul F. Cummins

COLUMBUS DAY?

I'm all for traditions. I like trick-or-treating on Halloween and exchanging gifts at Christmas and Channukah. I like birthday celebrations and celebrating genuine heroes like Abraham Lincoln and Martin Luther King Jr. But Christopher Columbus? What is it that we are celebrating on Columbus day? A historical lie? Genocide? The American Holocaust? We have the Fourth of July to celebrate our independence and President's Day to celebrate Washington and Lincoln. But Columbus? At the risk of seeming a spoilsport or grinch or iconoclast I think we should reconsider.

"In 1492 Columbus discovered America." Every school child memorizes this phrase, a phrase as seemingly American as apple pie. Nevertheless, there are complications here. In the first place, Eric the Red, Lief Ericson and other Norsemen arrived on the North American continent long before Columbus. If anybody not living here "discovered" America, the Vikings did. Second, Columbus died not knowing what he "discovered." And third, there were already millions of indigenous people living in the western hemisphere with rich cultures and traditions. So, in what sense did he "discover" America? In reality, what he did was stake a claim for white Europeans to murder and steal the lands of less well armed peoples. How can you "discover" a place where other people are already living?

On Columbus Day, what we are celebrating is the guy who made Europe aware of opportunities for plunder, exploitation, and expropriation. This is cause for a national holiday?

Let us, however, look a little further. What kind of a guy was this Italian navigator whom we revere as an American national hero? Let's turn to his journals for some clues. First of all, he was devoted to the acquisition of *gold*. In his 1492 journal, the word gold appears 75 times! Second, he was cruel: seeing bits of gold among the natives he assumed there were vast treasures available, so he ordered the natives to bring him quotas of gold. If they failed, he had their arms hacked off. Third, he was arrogant, assuming he had the right to impose his religion, Christianity, upon the natives who already had their own religions. Thus, we Americans who celebrate those forefathers who came to America to gain religious freedom, also celebrate an Italian forefather who robbed indigenous peoples of their religious freedom. And finally, as his journal reveals, he was an imperialist despot. Read, for example, this entry in his journal: "They [the natives] are simple and honest and exceedingly liberal with all they have, none of them refusing anything he may have when he is asked for it. They exhibit great love towards all others in preference to themselves. *They would*

6

make fine servants. With fifty men we could subjugate them all and make them do whatever we want. [italics mine]

Thereupon, Columbus and his men rounded up about 1,200 natives, selected 500, jammed them into boats and sent them off to Spain. About 200 died on the way. In Columbus' journal in 1498, he wrote: "From here one might send, in the name of the holy Trinity, as many slaves as could be sold." Consequently, Columbus, finding there was not as much gold among the natives as he had thought, substituted human slaves for gold as his bounty.

Greedy, cruel, arrogant, despotic, and a slaver–this is a guy we want to claim as a national hero?

Now certainly Columbus was a superb navigator and perhaps we could honor him along with other naval heroes and declare a NATIONAL NAVIGATIONAL HEROES HOLIDAY. But a day just for Christopher Columbus?

And, finally, what was Columbus' legacy? Hispaniola–a paradise in 1492, the island where Columbus landed (now Haiti and the Dominican Republic)–was populated by about 300,000 people. Between 1494 and 1496, approximately one-third were killed. Though we certainly cannot blame Columbus alone for the entire long disaster that befell the American Indians on the land ultimately stolen from them by the United States, it can be said with equal certainty that he began the process. The "process" ultimately encompassed European diseases, the introduction of guns, the liquor, and the scorched-earth policy of vengeful Euro-Americans, a process which led to millions of deaths of the indigenous peoples. The American Indians who numbered over five million in 1492, shrank to about 250,000 in 1890-1900.

So, let's find some new heroes to celebrate. Columbus is a lousy choice.

Paul F. Cummins

DUMB, DUMBER, DUMBEST: WATCHING PEOPLE SLEEP

My wife and I listened to Warren Olney's "Which Way LA" in stunned disbelief. And, as we were discussing the programs topic, our daughter breezed through the room and informed us that we were hopelessly "five minutes ago!" Translation: we were discussing old news. For Olney was talking about people logging in on the internet to watch a 23-year old woman (Jenny) filming herself—her every day-to-day, mundane activities—activities that netted her some 4.5-5 million internet hits per day. In fact, it turns out that people are actually watching her sleep. My 23-year old daughter had a simple explanation: most of the viewers were probably horny older men. Perhaps it's that simple. But Olney had several college professors on his show analyzing the cultural, sociological and psychological implications of this phenomenon of millions of people watching what they call "reality—as opposed to television programs which were edited, selected, and created." I mean why would you want to watch a Kurosawa or Bergman film when you can watch Jenny brush her teeth? Somehow this preference of "reality" to "art" seemed, to several commentators, to justify these viewers fascination with Jenny's day-to-day stuff.

My wife and I couldn't help but have a different take. Five million people watching someone sleep seemed to us yet another pathetic example of the dumbing down of America. From watered down text books (from college to grade school), to wrestling and the roller derby on television, to Jerry Springer, to sleep watching seems a continuum of dumb to dumber to even dumber. It seems that those people who are actually concerned that soap operas or even Jerry Springer are fabrications can then only turn to some other form of media to try to fill up their empty lives. Apparently it doesn't occur to any of these vidiots to turn off the screen and read or write or build or create something themselves, walk, meet a friend for coffee, whatever. No, they would prefer to watch someone sleep. As Don Imus would say, "Holy Mother of God..."

I don't know which was worse—the phenomenon Warren Olney described or the college professors trying to intellectualize some deeper meaning out of it. But what can you expect from dumbed down colleges. On the same day that I heard "Which Way LA," I heard a news clip of a college actually offering a course on "how to conduct business conversations on the golf course." Yes. An honest-to-god entire course brimmed full of insights such as, "don't discuss actual business until the seventh hole." My God, I thought, just think how rich and successful I might be if I had taken such a course in college. Problem is, I don't play golf. But perhaps I could have hired a stand-in to hit the golf balls while I walked along and engaged in conversation about potential business deals. Why not—we have services on many college campuses which provide ready made term papers for sale and we have Cliff notes to save you the trouble of actually reading a given book. And now, we have people sleeping on the internet so you can substitute their unconsciousness for your own consciousness. What a deal!

Paul F. Cummins

"$450,000 FOR SERVANTS' SUITES"

Just when you think you've heard it all, just when you think a given absurdity can't be topped, you get fooled! I mean, a Hollywood mogul will build a 50,000 square foot home and people will say, "Well, isn't that just about the limit?" But, of course, it isn't. Because you know that monuments to the human ego continue to proliferate and, as the gap between rich and poor widens, we can expect more and more grotesque forms of ostentation and conspicuous consumption.

Here's the latest: *"Sound like home, sweet home? Step right up, but only if you've got $100 million in assets to support your bid to live at 515 Park Avenue (NYC). This 43-story brick-and-limestone condominium will soon be home to some of the wealthiest people in the world–investment bankers and others whose stock market winnings will help pay $6 million to $15 million per apartment, plus $450,000 for servants' suites, $25,000 to store 1,000 bottles of wine, and an additional $4,000 in monthly fees."* (David Rynecki, *USA Today*, August 20, 1999).

Thorstein Veblen, where are you when we need you most? So while the homeless (including abandoned and abused children) and impoverished-unemployed men, women and their children wander the streets, these Park Avenue folks will be looking down upon them from their $15 million condos. What's wrong with this picture? What's more, who cares? Do any of us? Are we willing to let the gap widen and widen? Is it okay that American CEO's keep increasing the gulf between themselves and their workers, with the USA by far the leader in this hog ratio? (Note: in Germany, the salary ratio is 75:1; in the USA, it is over 400:1). Is this really what we mean by rugged individualism? The American way? Are we truly content to see our nation boast of such obscene discrepancies between the rich and the poor?

The advocates of unbridled capitalism will often respond, "If you don't like it, why don't you move to Russia?" Well, I don't want to live in Russia. I love this country. I work hard and I make a decent living here. I just would like to see some minimal effort at equity and fairness within the capitalist structure.

"And how would you propose to do this?" the advocates of unbridled greed will ask. So I suppose if I choose to complain about this or that, I ought to have an alternative to offer. So, in the interest of creating dialogue and suggesting potentially offensive suggestions, here are some alternatives.

One, we might consider a simple, progressive income tax. No loopholes. Just a simple principle: As you earn more, you always get to keep more that you earned at the previous level, but your tax rate goes up. At the 90% level, an individual earning one billion dollars in a given year gets to keep $1 hundred million, surely enough to make ends meet and enable that individual to squeak by for the year.

Second, eliminate some of the most glaring forms of corporate welfare, which even *Time Magazine* found indefensible. At the same time, we might restore corporate taxes to the level they were prior to the Reagan "Revolution"–I put the word revolution in quotes to indicate the upside-down use of the word in applying it to robbing the poor to increase the booty of the rich.

Third, we might re-examine our bloated defense spending and ask ourselves: against whom are we defending our nation? Might we not actually provide the poor with the peace dividend supposedly forthcoming just after the collapse of the Soviet Union? Perhaps we could spend this dividend on housing, cleaning-up inner cities, building new schools, job training, and the like. Curious, isn't it, that this "dividend" has been dropped from public parlance now that the economy is booming and now that greed seems to be the primary motivation of spending and investing?

Finally, I would like to see equity and fairness–i.e., providing the poor with a decent chance in our society–by increasing taxes on socially harmful products. Thus, I would want to see hefty taxes levied upon tobacco, guns and ammunition, liquor, and gasoline. Such taxes would not only increase revenue to reinvest in our inner cities, schools, and infrastructure, but would decrease spending on lung cancer, medical attention to victims of guns, alcohol abuse and automobile accidents. I am assuming that these taxes would decrease use of tobacco, guns, alcohol, and automobiles.

Clearly, there are many ways we could attack poverty in the United States. I keep hoping leaders in government and the private sector will emerge to point the way. I hope I don't spend the rest of my life waiting in vain for such leadership.

Paul F. Cummins

A SELF-DESTRUCTIVE ROAD

As a former Headmaster and current purveyor of educational reform, I am constantly involved in activities related to the F-word, that is, *fund raising*. I am, of course, often surprised and delighted by the generosity of various individuals, foundations and corporations. Nonetheless, I am also surprised and discouraged by the stinginess and self-absorption of some men and women of wealth. What amazes me is how many well-to-do people miss the opportunity to experience the excitement and satisfaction of giving. Certainly achieving, acquiring and amassing wealth have their gratifications, but it is ultimately an empty feeling compared to the joy of giving.

It is a strange fact that the old adage, "money cannot buy happiness" is so well documented and so little adhered to in people's lives. In a recent book on American culture (*The Real American Dream: A Meditation On Hope*), Andrew Delbanco quotes Herman Melville, "We become sad in the first place because we have nothing stirring to do." Making money is finally not stirring. As Debanco himself writes, "A merely secular project cannot, in the end, fend off melancholy." Yet the decades of the 80s and the 90s have "installed instant gratification as the hallmark of the good life." Delbanco doesn't offer solutions, but he seeks a humanistic commitment to social justice within a vague new relationship to the divine. Nevertheless, even if we live in a time of moral relativism, religious confusion, atheism, fatalism, and cynicism, it is clear that pure materialism and acquisitive consumerism are not answers to any of life's deeper questions. There is even now some research data to support the notion that money can't buy a sense of well-being. Two university researchers (Richard Ryan of the University of Rochester and Tim Kassner of Knox College) conducted a study in several cultures (including 12 countries) which concludes that pursuing wealth is psychologically unhelpful and often destructive. Living in an atmosphere where affluence is the focus runs counter to happiness, the researchers report. This is not exactly a startling discovery; we intuitively know it to be true. Now, it is also one that extensive research has proven to be valid.

While I haven't kept records or compiled well-organized data, my own experience of being a Headmaster/President of a private school for 32 years supports the Ryan/Kassner studies. I have known affluent and happy parents, but the happiness was always independent of the affluence; conversely, I have seen dozens and dozens of families dragged down and at times even destroyed by their inability to get beyond focusing upon the acquisition, possession of, and indulgence in their own wealth. Wealth was and is for many young people a curse, and for their parents can be a strange form of imprisonment which frequently renders even friendships and respect as suspicious–"do they really like me or do they just want my money?" Often I have seen money turn relatively normal and generous individuals into bizarrely stingy and fearful persons.

So what conclusions can we reach? An obvious one is that relationships are the domain in which happiness is to be found. The heart does not recognize cash value; it only recognizes essentials. As the little prince says in St. Exupery's classic, "That which is essential is invisible." Ego in the form of self-aggrandizement is doomed. So, it is in friendship, love, and compassion where happiness is to be found. A second conclusion is based on the New Testament dictum that it is more blessed to give than to receive. Ultimately, it is simply more fun as well. And, finally, it is clear, at least to me, that the contemporary obsession with possession endangers the future of humankind. Possession mania not only erodes private happiness–it threatens our very survival. Private ownership has gradually replaced communal sharing to the point where multitudes of children the globe over die every day of starvation while relatively few people amass huge private fortunes. "As private ownership becomes more widely accepted and the public sector loses influence, more and more of the world's wealth is now in private hands, where it fosters consumption that is outstripping global limits." (Gary Gardner, "Shared Destinies", *UTNE READER*, Nov.-Dec. 1999, p. 79.)

What does this have to do with giving and with philanthropy? Only this–that if we are to save the planet and achieve any equity among its peoples, we will have to move away from the notion that it is okay for the few to amass more and more of the world's resources and wealth. The ultimate acts of giving will have to be to give up this ego-centered, elitist, and exclusive vision of how to run the planet. We are currently traveling down a road where our activities are neither producing personal fulfillness for ourselves or a better life for others.

Paul F. Cummins

A CLUTTER OF FRIENDS

One of the sad realities of our times is the speed with which wonderful books come into print and disappear. Some are remaindered; some are warehoused; some show up in thrift-shops and used books stores; some find their way into libraries (though many never do, as library budgets shrink); many are simply returned to the publisher where they are shredded. Yes, publishers shred them rather than donating them to libraries or inner city or third world schools–it's cheaper to shred than to mail.

So, wonderful books come and go. They represent the dreams and sweat, months and years of labor of the dedicated writers. They come and they simply disappear.

Recently, I was reorganizing my own 40+ year accumulation of books and my wife was clearing my overflow out of her piano studio. "Why don't you get rid of at least some of these?" she asked me. But how could I do that to the writers, to these books–they are, in a real sense, friends. Each of them embodies memories and experiences. I remember where and when I bought this novel, that volume of poetry, why I bought it, classes I taught using this poem or that story for discussion. When I look across a shelf at titles, I remember friends who loved this or that book. My college friend, Jon Harris, who loved Unamuno's *Tragic Sense of Life*; Jon who plunged to his tragic death in Big Sur when his motorcycle went off a cliff. Or Phil Holmes, an extraordinary English teacher and friend who introduced me to C.S. Lewis' gem of a book, *The Abolition of Man*. Or my college roommate, John Carswell, who turned me on to Dylan Thomas, J.D. Salinger, and Andre Malraux.

Other shelves represent courses from my undergraduate years, courses from which I saved every assigned text and even the recommended supplementary reading which I acquired like an obsessed antique collector. Some, in fact, are antique books–or at least long since out-of-print: i.e., the complete works in English of Milovan Djilas; almost every book ever published of the 18th century British artist Thomas Rowlandson; the complete collection of poems by a minor poet Lew Sarett, who was my father's college professor in 1931 at Northwestern University.

Books aren't just books. They aren't just objects. They can be part of the fabric of our lives. They comfort us, inspire us, lead us into strange lands, open new worlds for us. So, for me, throwing them out is out of the question.

However, now that my life is statistically three-quarters over, I do ponder what their fate will be when I die. Somehow I want my children to keep them intact. It's almost as if I see them as a family not to be separated and dispersed, almost as if there is some mysterious relationship among them that someone in the future will comprehend and enjoy. This is, of course, pure fantasy and probably even silly, but the thought comforts me.

In the meanwhile, I build new book shelves, donate some books to the Crossroads School and New Roads School libraries, and rearrange some of the newer acquisitions in shelves with kindred volumes. Recently, for example, I read Neil Sheehan's extraordinary study of Vietnam, *A Bright Shining Lie*, and placed it beside by early editions of Bob Sheer's *Ramparts* magazine pamphlets, and added the recently published book by Denise Chong, *The Girl In the Picture*–the account of the little Vietnamese girl running up the road, crying in pain after being burned by a napalm attack.

I also have started to replenish a few formerly complete collections which have been depleted by loans never returned. For example, I just purchased *The Goodbye Look* and *The Moving Target* by Ross McDonald, my all-time favorite mystery writer. And, I picked up a new translation of *Don Quixote* by Burton Raffel to keep my English translation collection up to date.

I started this column intending to recommend a few out-or-print books to any interested reader but, as so often happens when pen hits paper, the article took a slightly different direction. Still, I highly recommend the books mentioned above, even if some are difficult to find. They are well worth the search. Perhaps some will even join your pantheon of irreplaceable friends.

WHO'S THE GREATEST?

Who's the greatest? Ty Cobb or Pete Rose? Tris Speaker or Joe Dimaggio? Babe Ruth or Hank Aaron? Who's the greatest American novelist–Melville or Fitzgerald? Hawthorne or Hemingway? The greatest American poet–Walt Whitman or Emily Dickinson? Williams or Eliot? Questions like these, particularly after a few beers or glasses of wine, often elicit stimulating arguments. Recently a group of friends and I argued the greatest American poet question. Predictably, Whitman and Dickinson were proffered first. I demurred and offered Robert Frost instead. To help my position, I threw in the desert island game as a supplementary question: which of the three (or any others) would you take to a desert island if you could choose only one? Here, I felt I had a trump card: Whitman would cloy after a while and Emily would drive you crazy with her quizzical and cryptic utterances. Frost, however, ranges widely from lyric to narrative, from folksy to philosophical, and his range would wear well on a desert isle. My companions had to agree that this was a convincing argument.

Actually, Frost no longer requires apologists, such is his reputation as one of America's greatest literary figures. Nonetheless, for those who haven't read him for a spell, I thought I would recite some of his most compelling characteristics. Years ago, the poet and critic John Ciardi said, "Robert Frost was no lollipop." Another critic, Lionell Trilling, referred to Frost as "a terrifying poet." Both were, I believe, countering the conventional misrepresentation of Frost as a sort of cracker barrel philosopher one reads while eating apple pie and sipping warm milk. There is an underlying darkness in Frost which is tough-minded. As he says in one of his poems: "I have been one acquainted with the night." Even when "the woods are lovely dark and deep," Frost brings the demands of reality to the forefront by reminding himself, and us, that, "I have promises to keep, and miles to go before I sleep." To emphasize the double nature of the journey, he repeats the last line – "and miles to go before I sleep."

R.W.B. Lewis once provided a framework to reflect upon the American experience. In his book, <u>The American Adam,</u> Lewis suggested that the concept of America as a new Eden, a new beginning where human nature could re-create itself far from the corrupting influences of Europe, was a pervasive and influential concept in American literature. Frequently, this new American (Adam) experienced a sense of freedom and liberation in the new world. Frost, however, is not so optimistic. In fact, in one of his distinctly Edenic poems, he presents the arrival of Eve as a mysterious presence who changes everything:

"Never again would the birds' song be the same.
And to do that to birds was why she came."

Frost looks back to Eden and sees not an original innocence, but a primal guilt. Truly he was no lollipop.

Perhaps Frost is confusing to some readers because he seems so simple, so folksy: "Good fences make good neighbors"... "Earth's the right place for love, I don't know where it's likely to go better"... "For I have had too much of apple-picking"... But in each of these famous poems–*Mending Wall, Birches,* and *After Apple Picking*–there are deeper meanings; there are, in fact, levels and levels one can attempt to penetrate and continue making new discoveries.

There is one short poem I would offer as quintessential Frost. *The Oven Bird* is, ostensibly, a nature poem. An oven bird, we find in the dictionary, is an American warbler (a good choice of bird for a poet to consider) that builds an oven-shaped nest of leaves, twigs, etc., on the forest floor. This fact provides Frost with his metaphor. Other birds build their nests up in the tree tops and they sing and twitter away in their beautiful voices during the spring and early summer and then fly south when it begins to get cold. The oven bird, however, has a raucous, unmelodic voice, builds his nest on the ground, and does not fly south when it gets cold. He stays and sings his unattractive songs in the late summer:

"He says that leaves are old and that for flowers
Mid-summer is to spring as one to ten"

He is unafraid to deal with either the falling of leaves, or the loss of the beautiful blossoms of spring. As summer gives way to fall he continues to deal with reality and with decline:

"And comes that other fall we name the fall.
He says the highway dust is over all."

Frost does in this poem (and in poem after poem) what great artists over the centuries have done. He takes the painful and difficult realities of mortality and converts them into beautiful works of art:

"The bird would cease and be as other birds
But that he knows in singing not to sing.
The question that he frames in all but words
Is what to make of a diminished thing."

Yes, Robert Frost is no lollipop.

Paul F. Cummins

FIFTY GREAT 20TH CENTURY NOVELS

Compiling lists of the best of this or that is always subjective and subject to debate which is probably why we enjoy compiling such lists. In the past year or so, there have been many lists of the best books of the 20th century. Most recently, <u>CONTEXTS</u>, a literary magazine from *Dalkey Archive Press* issued their list of major 20th century writers. So I decided to try my hand at it.

My criteria follow: 1) books I have actually read; 2) books of high writing style; 3) books of critical acclaim; 4) books of historical importance (i.e., consciousness raising); and 5) books that in many cases influenced other writers and readers. This is a two-part series of articles beginning with 50 great novels. The second article will focus on non-fiction. My lists are admittedly idiosyncratic, non-prioritized, and personal; here goes.

James Joyce, <u>Portrait of the Artist as a Young Man</u>
James Joyce, <u>Ulysses</u>
Thomas Mann, <u>The Magic Mountain</u>
F. Scott Fitzgerald, <u>The Great Gatsby</u>
Ernest Hemingway, <u>The Sun Also Rises</u>
Mikhail Sholokov, <u>And Quiet Flows the Don</u>
Boris Pasternak, <u>Doctor Zhivago</u>
Upton Sinclair, <u>The Jungle</u>
Eli Weisel, <u>Night</u>
Jerzy Kosinski, <u>The Painted Bird</u>
Erich Maria Remarque, <u>All Quiet on the Western Front</u>
Albert Camus, <u>The Stranger</u>
Andre Malraux, <u>Man's Fate</u>
John Steinbeck, <u>The Grapes of Wrath</u>
George Orwell, <u>1984</u>
George Orwell, <u>Animal Farm</u>
Chinua Achebe, <u>Things Fall Apart</u>
J.D. Salinger, <u>Catcher in the Rye</u>
John Hersey, <u>Hiroshima</u>
Ralph Ellison, <u>Invisible Man</u>
William Faulkner, <u>The Sound and the Fury</u>
Robert Penn Warren, <u>All the Kings Men</u>
E.M. Forster, <u>A Passage to India</u>
Joseph Heller, <u>Catch-22</u>
Kurt Vonnegut, <u>Slaughterhouse-five</u>
Joseph Conrad, <u>Lord Jim</u>

Joseph Conrad, <u>Heart of Darkness</u>
William Styron, <u>Sophie's Choice</u>
Edith Wharton, <u>The Age of Innocence</u>
D.H. Lawrence, <u>Sons and Lovers</u>
Franz Kafka, <u>The Trial</u>
Arthur Koestler, <u>Darkness At Noon</u>
Alexander Solzhenitsyn, <u>One Day in the Life of Ivan Denisovich</u>
John Dos Passos, <u>USA Trilogy</u>
Leslie Marmon Silko, <u>Ceremony</u>
N. Scott Momaday, <u>House Made of Dawn</u>
William Gaddis, <u>The Recognitions</u>
Sinclair Lewis, <u>Main Street</u>
Hermann Hesse, <u>Siddhartha</u>
Joseph Roth, <u>Radetzky March</u>
Richard Wright, <u>Native Son</u>
Carlo Levi, <u>Christ Stopped at Eboli</u>
Graham Greene, <u>The Quiet American</u>
D.M. Thomas, <u>The White Hotel</u>
Gabriel Garcia Marquez, <u>One Hundred Years of Solitude</u>
Thomas Keneally, <u>Schindler's List</u>
Iris Murdoch, <u>The Black Prince</u>
Gilbert Sorrentino, <u>Mulligan Stew</u>
Philip Roth, <u>The Great American Novel</u>
Robert Coover, <u>The Universal Baseball Machine</u>

After compiling this list, I waited a few days and tried to look at it with an objective eye. A couple things struck me: it is heavily a Western-European list and it is heavily a white male list. Not surprising, since both are my heritage. An Egyptian or African or Peruvian would, no doubt, compile a different list. Nonetheless, given the criteria I imposed on myself, this is, I believe, a good list to stimulate discussion.

I can certainly say that every book on the list makes for wonderful reading. Some are utterly terrifying–<u>Night</u>, <u>Sophie's Choice</u>, <u>The Painted Bird</u>, <u>Hiroshima</u>; others are hilarious–<u>Mulligan Stew</u>, <u>The Great American Novel</u>; others are stylistic tour de forces–<u>The Sound and the Fury</u>, <u>Ulysses</u>, <u>The Recognitions</u>, <u>The White Hotel</u>; and others so capture the 20th century landscape that they not only give perspective to the century, but actually help to define it–<u>1984</u>, <u>Heart of Darkness</u>, <u>Catch 22</u>, <u>The Grapes of Wrath</u>, <u>The Trial</u>, <u>The Stranger</u>, and <u>Invisible Man</u>. And, finally, some are simply instant classics which beautifully combine all the elements of story, style, and content. These would include <u>The Magic Mountain</u>, <u>Doctor Zhivago</u>, <u>Sons and Lovers</u>, and <u>All The Kings Men</u>.

Paul F. Cummins

I welcome responses from any interested readers.

THE FIFTY GREATEST 20TH CENTURY NOVELS REVISITED

Writing a column in a newspaper sometimes feels like putting notes in bottles and sending them off to sea. You don't know what response–if any–they are engendering. However, I had two pleasant experiences recently. I met a Seattle's Best (coffee shop) regular (Michelle Topham) who told me she had enjoyed my column from December 28th called FIFTY GREAT 20TH CENTURY NOVELS, and was reading all fifty–one a day! She is now on book seven (<u>1984</u> by Orwell).

Then I received an extraordinarily thoughtful letter from reader Jeffrey Graham which I offer here in lieu of my regular column, because I think it represents the kind of dialogue writers hunger for and rarely receive:

January 2, 2001
RE: Fifty Great 20th Century Novels

Dear Paul:

I share your fascination with literature. The temptation to respond to your "Santa Monica Mirror" article was as sweet as the Dutch chocolate drops we've been plying for the holidays. It also serves as an elegant excuse to make contact with you, as I have been admiring your work from afar: educational and journalistic, and would enjoy the opportunity to meet with you. More on that later. First, the books:

1. *Your selection of numerous texts with a decidedly social and daresay socialist leaning is telegraphed by your parenthetical: "consciousness-raising" within the criteria section. I don't argue with your choices of <u>The Jungle, All Quiet, The Grapes,</u> nor <u>Main Street</u>. Personally I appreciate your tilt towards these anti-war/anti-establishment works, and the fact that you certify your 50 as such attests to your integrity. In my own pantheon of greatest 50, however, there are a few on my list that must bump some of yours, with casualties counted among those more political in favor of the more "literary" from my standpoint.*

2. *The great Thomas Wolfe is a most glaring omission. I suggest <u>Look Homeward Angel</u>, though my personal favorites are <u>You Can't Go Home Again</u> and <u>The Web and the Rock</u>. Wolfe was influential upon many a small town Southern writer, including William Styron. Wolfe was incredibly*

lyrical, full of epiphany, with uniquely American themes. He was greatly influenced by James Joyce.

3. *I can't help but notice your list begins with twin Joycean texts, with which I concur. However, you make no mention of the prioritization of the 50. Is it true that your choices are presented in descending order of importance? Seems so. Coincidentally, your first five choices parallel my own top five. Isn't that swell?*

4. *Displaying my ignorance, I simply don't know and therefore can't comment upon <u>And Quiet Flows the Don, Things Fall Apart, Ceremony,</u> and <u>House Made of Dawn</u>.*

5. *You reveal a cinemagraphic sensibility with your choices of <u>Zhivago, Slaughterhouse Five, A Passage to India,</u> and <u>Shindler's List</u>. Certainly these books greatly influenced the public once they entered the popular culture through film. Such films foster a cross-pollenization that might have occurred as well with <u>Beloved</u> but did not though it deserves a broader audience, and appears on my list.*

6. *Thank you for including the holocaust literature you did. I make one further recommendation, suggested by your selection of Carlo Levi's book: Primo Levi's <u>Survival in Auschwitz</u> originally entitled <u>If This is a Man</u>, which you may also include on your non-fiction list. (I don't know the Carlo Levi, and can't comment on that one.)*

7. *I question the need to include both Orwell texts, particularly when Faulkner has only one. I would tend to favor Huxley's <u>Brave New World</u> over one or the other Orwell. It's so darned presumptuous to get non-committal on such a project as this.*

8. *Are <u>Hiroshima, The Quiet American,</u> and <u>Darkness at Noon</u> generational? I am 43 and may have just missed them. I've heard of them but not in this context.*

9. *Your inclusion of Dos Passos somehow invites me to consider other post WWI texts and their writers that I associate with the American identity and American modernism: Gertrude Stein's <u>The Autobiography of Alice B. Toklas</u> or <u>Lectures in America</u>, and W.C. Williams' <u>In the American Grain</u>. The former is more the grammararian and the latter the poet through they both deserve elevated placements in the canon in my view.*

10. *I treasure Iris Murdoch, Roth and Coover as authors, and it pleases me that they make it on. There is a wonderful Roth book from the early 70s that I recently discovered called <u>My Life as A Man</u>. I particularly enjoyed Coover's pseudo-auto-biographical spoof on Nixon.*

11. *Authors missing in action; Virginia Woolf (<u>To the Lighthouse</u> or <u>Mrs. Dalloway</u>), John Barth (<u>Chimera</u> or <u>Lost in the Funhouse</u>), Saul Bellow (<u>Henderson the Rain King</u> or <u>Herzog</u>), not to mention these seminal texts: <u>Moby-Dick, Huck Finn, Red Badge of Courage,</u> and <u>The Scarlet Letter</u>.*

Thank you for this wonderful new year's diversion. It's a pleasure.

Thank you, Jeffrey and I hope other readers will follow suit.

Paul F. Cummins

"WHAT A WONDERFUL WORLD"

So, as Louis Armstrong sings, "and I say to myself, what a wonderful world..." Yes, folks, it's a wonderful world. Why just consider these little selections:

- 1.6 billion people are worse off now than they were 15 years ago;
- One Mexican billionaire is as rich as 17 million Mexicans;
- Of every 10 poor people, seven are women;
- 17 million Africans have died since the AIDS epidemic began in the late 1970s–more than 3.7 million of them children;
- In Botswana, Swaziland, Zimbabwe, Lesotho, Zambia, South Africa and Namibia at least one adult in five is living with HIV;
- Americans constitute less than 5% of the world's population, but consume nearly 25% of the world's energy;
- Less than 2% of Europe's forests are left in their original state, untouched or replanted by man;
- The 200 richest individuals in the world have more assets than the 2 billion poorest;
- Each day in developing nations, an estimated 250 million children focus on going to work instead of going to school, making goods that profit global corporations.

Sing it, Louis: "and I say to myself, what a wonderful world." But let's continue:

- For every 100 pounds of product we manufacture in the United States, we create 3,200+ pounds of waste;
- Between 1900 and 1984 the USA junked 647 million automobiles and trucks;
- The American auto industry spends $14 billion a year persuading Americans to buy cars;
- The world's 200 largest corporations account for 27.5% of global economic activity; they employ 0.8% of the world's population;

"And I say to myself..."

- In 1995, there were 77 homicides with guns in England; there were 13,673 in America;

- Since 1940, the U.S. has spent (in 1996 dollars) over 5.5 trillion dollars on nuclear weapons;
- A new 43 story condo in New York is selling suites ranging from 6 million (on the low end) to 15 million each;
- Each day on planet earth over 20,000 children die of malnutrition and starvation.

"...what a wonderful world."

Paul F. Cummins

FIFTY GREAT 20TH CENTURY WORKS OF NON-FICTION

Because my article on fifty great novels of the 20th century generated a surprising response from readers, I decided to try it again–this time with fifty works of non-fiction.

My list is admittedly idiosyncratic and reflective of my own interests in history, politics, literature, and social reform. It is, also, as a friend pointed out, a bit skimpy on works of science and technology. I also excluded biography just to reduce the boundaries.

This list, by the way, is not prioritized or even alphabetized. It is a somewhat random list, but I hope it will provoke readers to think of their own favorites and, perhaps, to read a few from this list of fifty.

Rachel Carson, <u>Silent Spring</u>
Jared Diamond, <u>Guns, Germs and Steel</u>
Noam Chomsky, <u>Deterring Democracy</u>
Simone De Beauvior, <u>The Second Sex</u>
George Orwell, <u>Essays</u>
Eduardo Galeano, <u>Masks of Fire</u> (a trilogy)
Milovan Djilas, <u>The New Class</u>
Jonathan Kozol, <u>Savage Inequalities</u>
J.P. Sartre, <u>Existentialism and Human Emotions</u>
Thomas Berry, <u>The Dream of the Earth</u>
Pierre Teilhard de Chardin, <u>The Phenomenon of Man</u>
Alexander Solzhenitzyn, <u>The Gulag Archipelago</u>
C.S. Lewis, <u>The Abolition of Man</u>
Gunnar Myrdal, <u>An American Dilemma</u>
John Muir, <u>The Yosemite</u>
Eric Goldman, <u>Rendezvous With Destiny</u>
Alfred Kazin, <u>On Native Grounds</u>
Reinhold Niebuhr, <u>Children of Light and Children of Darkness</u>
C.J. Jung, <u>Modern Man in Search of a Soul</u>
Michael Harrington, <u>The Other America</u>
Albert Schweitzer, <u>Out Of My Life and Thought</u>
Albert Camus, <u>Resistance, Rebellion and Death</u>
Paul Tillich, <u>The Courage To Be</u>
John Dewey, <u>Democracy and Education</u>
Martin Luther King, Jr., <u>Collected Speeches</u>
William Shirer, <u>The Rise and Fall of the Third Reich</u>
Dee Brown, <u>Bury My Heart At Wounded Knee</u>

Jonathan Schell, The Fate of the Earth
Neil Sheehan, A Bright Shining Lie
Richard Hofstader, The American Political Tradition
John Kenneth Galbraith, The New Industrial State
James Baldwin, The Fire Next Time
Hannah Arendt, Eichmann in Jerusalem
Alfred Korzybski, Science and Sanity
Erick Erickson, Childhood and Society
Andre Malraux, The Voices of Silence
Sigmund Freud, Civilization and Its Discontents; An Interpretation of Dreams
Erich Fromm, Escape From Freedom
Karl Menninger, Man Against Himself
Jose Ortega y Gasset, The Revolt of the Masses
Truman Capote, In Cold Blood
Eugen Herrigel, Zen and The Art of Archery
Loren Eisley, The Immense Journey
Charles Beard, An Economic Interpretation of the Constitution
Erich Auerbach, Mimesis
William Barrett, Irrational Man
William James, Varieties of Religious Experience
Martin Buber, I And Thou
George Gamov, The Creation of the Universe
Cleanth Brooks & Robert Penn Warren, Understanding Poetry

EDUCATION

TOWARD A MORE PLURALISTIC, HARMONIOUS NATION

When I was growing up, the concept of America as a "melting pot" was something to brag about. Now, however, the ideal of the melting pot–of stirring the admixture of diversity into a homogeneous soup–is no longer tenable even if it were desirable–which few today would advocate. The more likely and exciting prospect is the creation of a "new society" in which separate cultural identities are preserved while at the same time each becomes a strand into a new tapestry–a pluralistic nation that shares its diverse stories and values. This presumes communication among all the different cultural, ethnic, and international identities comprising this new America. It would also require a common language, English. Thus, while I argue for the necessity of each separate group to maintain its own language (how else could it preserve its stories?), I would argue equally strongly that each child *master* English. By master I mean achieve fluency, ease, and complexity of expression–both written and spoken. If we cannot educate all children in our common language, the Euro-centric opponents of multiculturalism (i.e., Arthur Schlesinger, Jr.) will have a field day. They charge that multiculturalism creates divisiveness, fragmentation, geographic and cultural isolation, exclusionism, and the loss of any common heritage–all these and more will be forcefully disseminated. The only way multiculturalism will achieve productive acceptance is if all children to learn English. Already, multiculturalism and multilingualism (in America) are regarded with suspicion and, often, outright hostility. WASPs and civic leaders see their country changing under their very eyes. In California, Texas, Illinois, Florida, and New York, the changes have been unprecedented. Thus, a retrenchment into "good old-fashioned American values" is to be expected. But the conservative approach, if modified by intelligent liberalism, can lead to mutually desired results.

First of all, we need to continue some bilingual acclimatization for immigrant children, with the understanding that mastery of their native language is not only an end in itself, but is the principal means of leading them to a mastery of English. Simply dropping a non-English speaking immigrant student into an all-English speaking class is unrealistic and unfair. Some explanation in one's native language is necessary to bridge the gap.

Second, increased funds must be raised in order to continue to lower class sizes; to provide teacher training and enrichment; and to hire more qualified bilingual teachers. If bilingualism and monolingualism (English) are not effective, the reason is the same as why math, science, and history teachers are ineffective. It has nothing to do with the subject–it has everything to do with class size, teaching conditions, neighborhood deterioration, and the like. We cannot put forty non-English speaking students from many language backgrounds in an English class and expect much progress. Thus, one way to improve students' English skills is to sensibly reform intolerable teaching conditions.

Third, I suggest that we provide at least one year of intensive English for ESL students. One year. Six hours a day. Will this be costly? Yes and no. The costs can be mitigated by postponing–for one year–instruction of other subjects and simply focusing on English. In the long run, a student who speaks and writes English well is more likely to do well in school, not to drop out, not to join the ranks of the alienated and, hence, less likely to join gangs, engage in criminal activities, and finally, less likely to become part of the incredibly costly prison system.

Let's assume for the moment that we as a nation are dedicated to improving all classrooms, and especially English-language teaching conditions. To start, our teaching of history must be more compelling. Certainly the story of the white European colonists, the white male leaders of the Revolution, the framers of the Constitution and the captains of industry, inventors, foreign adventurers, el.al., is an essential thread of American history. But it is not the whole story. It omits the stories of women, as told by, experienced by, interpreted by, and written by women. The white European male story also omits or slants the Native American stories; the stories of Spanish and Mexican settlers and immigrants; the stories of Chinese laborers and other Asian immigrants: and, of course it distorts the stories of African-American slaves and the subsequent evolution of the blacks experience in America. Each of these stories is independent of, and interdependent with, the others. A rich fusion of music, art, political aspiration and achievement, intermarriage, conflict, injustices and triumphs–they are all part of a New Story we could as a nation recreate. The Baha'i faith proclaims that "the earth is but one country, and mankind its citizens." It would be a stunning achievement if the United States of America adopted this principle within its own borders.

Finally, I do not believe that a common language and an inclusive study of histories are by themselves enough to achieve a united country. There is another piece that is essential: we cannot achieve unity if our schools and neighborhoods remain segregated with "savage inequalities." The next generation of citizens and leaders cannot communicate and create community if they remain apart in rich enclaves and poor ghettoes attending segregated schools which, for the vast majority of minority children, means being relegated to underfunded, dilapidated, wholly inadequate schools.

There exists an interrelationship of all of our educational and social problems. In this case, multiculturalism is not a villain, but a blessing waiting to be received. The real villains are poverty, greed, selfishness, insensitivity, fear, exclusivity, xenophobia, racism, snobbery, elitism, and the like. Children are not natural adherents to this sad and sorry list. We teach them to be so. What a thrilling prospect it would be, just once, to teach a generation of children to respect and honor differences, to welcome change, and to seek to create newer and richer histories of America.

Paul F. Cummins

PRIVATE PARTNERSHIPS WITH PUBLIC SCHOOLS

Crossroads School devotes 10% of its operating budget to financial aid which this year (2001/02) is over $2 million. This helps the school to achieve a higher rate of diversity than most private schools in the state. Nevertheless, the Los Angeles Times constantly refers to Crossroads as a "westside elitist school." While Crossroads is certainly on the westside, its orientation and values are distinctly non-elitist.

I have chosen this subject not to brag about Crossroads, but to illustrate how a private school can serve the greater community. In fact, I believe that the private sector can be a major player in school reform, not only in Los Angeles, but also state and nation-wide. If every substantial private school–both pre-collegiate and collegiate–in the country made a concerted effort to share resources with public schools in their neighborhoods, they would make a huge, positive impact. Crossroads has made such an impact. Allow me to offer three illustrations.

First, ten years ago, Crossroads allowed me to change my role from day-to-day Headmaster to President of the school, focusing on community outreach. Our first act was to create a new non-profit corporation, The Crossroads Community Foundation (CCF) whose mission is to restore the arts to local public schools. CCF raises money to hire arts teachers and buy supplies and instruments. CCF literally gives those teachers' services to the public schools. This year, CCF is providing $1 million in instruction and arts experiences to twelve L.A.U.S.D. campuses. As a result of this, 4,000 children a week receive music, visual arts, dance, drama, and creative writing classes offered at every grade level for most of the school year, in a skill building and sequential program. CCF has, over the past ten years, provided over four million dollars to these same public schools. My salary and time as Executive Director was fully funded by Crossroads.

A second achievement of this "westside elitist school" is the creation of the New Visions Foundation (NVF) whose mission is to start new schools devoted to diversity, social justice, and environmental sanity. New Roads now has three campuses with 350 students. Over 40% of the operating budget goes for financial aid, and 60% of the students receive financial aid. This represents an extraordinary commitment to aid and diversity. In fact, 60% of New Roads student body is non-white. The students are demonstrating on a daily basis that integration works and works well. New Roads operates a middle school (grades 6-7-8) at the Santa Monica Boys/Girls Club, a middle school (6-7-8) at La Cienega and Rodeo Road in Baldwin Hills, and a high school (9-12) on Olympic Boulevard just west of Centinela.

In summary, Crossroads has assisted in providing the arts to twelve public school campuses and in creating three new campuses of New Roads–which is itself clearly not an elitist school.

The third illustration involves a unique three-way partnership. In this instance, Crossroads pays a salary for me to help launch a new charter (public) schools. To date, we have created four campuses, two elementary and two middle school, of a school called Camino Nuevo Charter Academy. The three partners are the New Visions Foundation, ExEd, and Pueblo Nuevo. Pueblo is a church founded by the Reverend Philip Lance, an inspired minister in the McArthur Park area. ExEd, headed by Bill Siart and his remarkable colleagues Anita Landecker, David Balsam, Cindy Seymour, and Nicole Harris, is a non-profit organization dedicated to creating and helping to financially manage new charter schools. New Visions Foundation is supplying the educational leadership. Together we bought an abandoned mini-mall near 7th and Alvarado: the Santa Monica architectural firm of Daly, Genik has designed the remodel, and we opened in August of 2000 with 260 children. During the time that we were remodeling the mini-mall, we secured a second elementary campus behind a hotel, an empty pre-school, so we added this to our elementary charter and opened it also in August of 2000 with 130 additional students. In August of 2001, we opened two new middle school campuses with over 600 students. We believe this is a model for the creation of other new schools.

So, these are the results of one westside non-elite school with a vision of the private sector serving a wider community. It is a model I hope to see replicated.

Paul F. Cummins

STANDARDS - WHOSE AND FOR WHAT?

We hear much about "standards" these days. We need standards, tough, challenging standards, high academic standards, college preparatory standards. Those invoking the phrase generally feel good in doing so. It makes the "standards"-advocates feel tough, demanding and academic. Never mind that believing in standards is a sort of motherhood statement. I mean who really does *not* believe in standards? Has any of us ever heard an educator, politician or civic leader say: "I *don't* believe in standards; I believe in a flabby, weak education that will not really prepare anyone for anything, much less for college." Since everyone believes in standards, the real issues are: What standards? Designed by whom and to what end?

Adolf Eichmann and Josef Goebbels could read and write well; they were good students; they went to college. They would have met the academic standards that educational standards-pushers are pushing today. Clearly standards are not an end in themselves. Reading and writing well are not valuable skills if they are applied to the propaganda of racism and genocide. Mathematical and statistical skills are not valuable if put to the purpose of calculating the extermination rates any given gas chamber can accomplish.

We all believe that certain academic, rational or logical thinking skills are important. But they are important only if they are informed by kindness and compassion, a sense of equity and justice, a care for the earth and its resources. In other words, standards without the deepest human values are not only *not* valuable, they can be dangerous and even destructive. Human history is littered with the tragic stories of innocent people maimed, tortured, and murdered by tyrants and power brokers who were themselves well educated–that is, the tyrants and their toadies who met the "educational standards" of the day.

I would urge, as our society indulges itself in the "feel-good" rhetoric of standards, that the word does not put thought to sleep. I put forth the notion that academic skills are tools whose use needs to be informed by higher standards– standards such as love, pity, compassion, justice, beauty, equity. This, of course, raises an enormously difficult question: How do you teach, inculcate, transmit such values? And, how do you do this without bringing religion into the schools and without violating the Constitutional requirement to keep church and state separate? I believe it can be done.

I believe that we can bring students into dialogues and experiences with the deepest human concerns of our times. In fact, I believe students hunger–as do adults–for meaning. Telling students they must meet academic standards to move to the next grade, to do well on standardized tests, to get into college, etc., does not give them a sense of purpose. They see through the shallowness of such supposed "ends." However, when students are confronted with real issues, with opportunities to become engaged in truly meaningful activities, then they want to meet the standards held before them, for when they are engaged, the skills that standards demand now seem to have a purpose.

Consequently, I believe that there are four areas where higher standards can be taught and in ways which fully engage young people These areas are: 1) community service activities (which can also have a demanding academic component); 2) environmental studies (including field trips, hiking and camping expeditions–which also can involve math, geography, map reading, astronomy, etc.); 3) the arts (the value of which is by now incontrovertible); and 4) human development programs (which can also cover the sciences through drug and sex education, physiology, conflict resolution, tolerance and co-existence education). These four areas are experiential and much of the learning is "hands-on." These four areas *engage* young people. I have witnessed this during forty years of teaching and administration. I know it to be true.

While we preach the importance of academic standards, let's also elevate the discussion to ask, standards to what ends? How can we engage young people in the life of their school and community? How can we incorporate standards not just to pass tests, but to inspire young people to seek real meaning in their lives and to help others upon this human journey? Evan S. Connell writes:

Each life is a myth, a song given out of darkness, a tale for children, the legend we create. Are we not heroes, each of us in one fashion or another, wandering through mysterious labyrinths?

Let's not forget, in the standards and test-score feeding frenzy that we now see all around us that life is dark and beautiful and mysterious, and that students know when their teachers and schools are confronting these deeper concerns. They will meet more and more demanding standards as we join with them in confronting issues that truly matter.

Paul F. Cummins

IN DEFENSE OF LATE BLOOMERS

I think I was fortunate to have grown up in the '30s, and '40s (I was born in 1937) and to attend high school and college in the 1950s. In the decade of the '50s the College Board Scores (SAT's) did not exercise such inordinate weight in determining a young person's future. Neither did grade point averages (GPA) nor advance placement tests (AP's). The competition for admissions into the highly selective colleges was not at the fever pitch it is today. Colleges had no quasi-objective reasons to deny this or that student. The triumvirate SAT-GPA-AP that now rules was then weak or non-existent. Consequently, there was ample time to grow, to wander down backroads, to enjoy the salad days of youth, to play kick-the-can and stick ball, and time to be carefree. Kids like me had a chance to grow up at their own pace.

I look back and realize now that I was a slow learner, a late bloomer, and, finally, an over-achiever. However, I was allowed the time to be all of those. I didn't hit my stride intellectually until mid-college; I needed time to learn how to learn and I needed time to discover myself and my passions. It was my good fortune to grow up when and where I was allowed this time. I feel sorry for kids today. How many of them, I wonder, are like me, but do not have the leisure to find themselves without feeling bad about themselves?

I remember, in particular, one incident that occurred after I graduated from college and which serves as food for thought. I was twenty-five years old, teaching at my old high school and feeling pretty good about myself. One day, I was looking for some alumni records and I came across my own file. And there they were...my SAT scores. I can honestly say, I had no recollection of ever having seen them before, or, even if I had, would I have known their significance. I was admitted to Stanford in 1955 when SAT's were relatively unimportant, and I never paid any attention to them.

Now, at age twenty-five, as a teacher, a college graduate (B.A., Stanford; M.A.T., Harvard) and a Ph.D. candidate at USC, here I was confronting my SAT scores for the first time. I was utterly shocked! They were amazingly low. I stared at the scores in disbelief, because now I was also a college counselor and understood their significance. I was depressed for weeks. Was I really that stupid? How could I be teaching when all my students were more intelligent? For a time I felt thoroughly disheartened. And yet, I was 25 years old, self-confident and successful in my chosen field. Nevertheless, these numbers hit me between the eyes.

How much more, I wonder, do younger students wilt under the societal weight of scores and grades? How many students, I wonder, fail to live up to their potential because a test score or grade fixes upon them a crippling self-image? How many potentially productive students do not produce because they have been led to feel inadequate? Some will discover, later, by accident or the good fortune of an encouraging teacher, that intelligence is as diverse as is the planet and that no one form of intelligence is the most important.

Our jobs as educators is to continually widen our vision of what intelligence is and how we can teach to the variety of young people before us. Our jobs as parents entails valuing the uniqueness of each child and endowing them the sense of self-respect and self-worth that allows for maximum growth. e.e. cummings once said he had a firm conviction "that nothing measurable is worth a good god damn."

Now, as President and a founder of Crossroads School, I am thankful that I never saw my SAT scores when I was 17 years old. If I had, Crossroads School would probably not exist.

TAKING THE SCHOOLS TO THE CHILDREN

I recently attended a groundbreaking conference at the Getty Center that was aimed at developing new perspectives to this problem. The conference, "New Schools, Better Neighborhoods," was organized by David Abel and Steve Soboroff, both civic leaders and members of the Citizens Committee on Proposition BB. It was historic for California bringing together leaders from all areas of city life–citizens' groups, officials from the Los Angeles Unified School District (L.A.U.S.D.), the Mayor's office, city government, architects and state government leaders to consider how we can create innovative designs for schools, designs that will be responsive to neighborhood needs and desires, and that are feasible–given government requirements and restrictions. This appears to be a huge, and at first glance, a seemingly impossible task.

Let's backtrack for a minute to place this conference topic within the historic moment:

–L.A.U.S.D. is bursting at the seams; Los Angeles needs to build 85 new schools ASAP!

–It now takes about five years to get a new school built.

–The overcrowded areas are desperately short of available acreage for new schools with playgrounds, parking, gyms, etc.

–The L.A.U.S.D. and state requirements for the process of selecting a new school comprise a list about as long as the income tax code.

Consequently, we are at a place in time where new schools needs to be created fast, yet the rules are ponderous and the space unavailable. What do we do?

Conventional thinking would require condemning dozens of homes, apartment buildings and stores, and relocating these folks–a costly, politically divisive, time-consuming matter. In fact, at the Getty Center Conference, members of the L.A.U.S.D. real estate department presented a case study showing how they could create a new school in the Cahuenga Elementary area by condemning properties. Another old way of thinking dictates the following formula: a high school should encompass over 3,600 youngsters, a middle school over 1,800, and an elementary school over 1,000.

The Conference suggested some new approaches. One is to create new schools on a smaller scale: more schools with fewer children, on smaller plots of land. A second case study was presented to illustrate how this could be done.

The study, the proposed Camino Nuevo Charter Academy, is a project that I have been working on since the last summer of 2000. Briefly, the Camino Nuevo plan, is to start an elementary school (K-5) of 240 students in an empty mini-mall in the McArthur Park neighborhood. Reverend Philip Lance, an imaginative Episcopal priest, who had started a store-front church and then two businesses with his parishioners, was approached by neighbors to help them start a new school. They were dissatisfied with their local school, which had recently ranked in the 9th percentile on state scores. Reverend Lance then approached me, and our foundation–the New Visions Foundation, d.b.a. New Roads School–to provide educational leadership. A third partner became ExEd, a Santa Monica-based private organization headed by Bill Siart, Former President of First Interstate Bank. ExEd provides financial management and expertise in creating charter schools.

Camino Nuevo Charter Academy will be devoted to developing English literacy within a Crossroads School/New Roads School philosophy of educating the whole child. In terms of space use, it will utilize existing space. Moreover, it will not dislocate or relocate anyone; it will be for neighborhood children, not bused-in kids; it will take advantage of neighborhood resources–parks, libraries, etc.

We think this is the right model for many new schools. This method is less expensive and can be used more quickly. Philip Lance, Bill Siart, and I plan to open the Camino Nuevo Charter Academy in September 2000, making this a 24-month process from concept to turnkey. Furthermore, many studies have shown that smaller is better. Small schools allow for a greater sense of community, more personal relations for every group of constituents–teachers, administrators, students and parents–and small allows for greater accountability and more accurate assessment.

Ironically, I think that necessity taught me many of these design lessons years ago. A group of us created Crossroads School in 1971-72. We did not have enough funds to buy a big campus, so we leased one building (Motherhood Maternity Warehouse, interestingly enough) on 21st Street in Santa Monica, and, in subsequent years, bought or leased 13 other properties, including an auto body shop, a machine shop, and two empty apartment buildings. We displaced no one. For 28 years, our school did not have a gym (finally, we opened one in 2000), yet during those first years, we won two state championships and six CIF championships in boys' basketball. We simply used community gyms and parks.

One of the clear messages coming out of the Getty conference was that we need to be more imaginative in the coming century to solve our problems, and that government and civic agencies, public and private groups, and citizen groups will need to cooperate and cut though existing red tape. As daunting as that may seem, I think we can do it, but only school by school, one small school at a time.

GRADUATION

All across the country in June (2000), graduation speakers wax poetic, ecstatic, pessimistic, optimistic, and nostalgic. Some speakers berate this generation, others place the future hopes of mankind upon their shoulders. They all, however, have one thing in common: they are eminently forgettable.

This year, I will deliver five (Crossroads 5th, 8th, 12th grades; New Roads 8th and 12th grades) of these forgettable addresses. So, lest any of my readers escape the imposition of a graduation speech, I offer one of my five to include readers in this annual ritual. Somewhat arbitrarily, I offer the New Roads 8th grade speech as my column for this week.

Hello everyone. I want to thank Chris Elder [Director of the New Roads Middle School in Santa Monica] and Charletta Johnson [Director of the New Roads Middle School at the La Cienega Campus] for inviting me here today, and I want to thank Chris and Charletta also for their superb leadership and wonderful spirit. Chris and Charletta are truly New Roads treasures.

To the 8th grade, I offer my congratulations and my happiness that we will have a wonderful new home, at our Herb Alpert campus, for many of you to come to in the 9th grade.

Today I want to talk to you–briefly–about magic in education. The HARRY POTTER fantasy series is a remarkable new addition to the world of children's classics. In these books, we meet Harry Potter, a young boy who is a wizard. His parents were killed by the evil Lord Voldemort when Harry was a child. But Harry escaped and he possesses magical powers he is only beginning to learn about. And, like all young heroes, he has to go through a period of education and initiation–like all of you potential young wizards.

So Harry goes off to the Hogwarts School for Witchcraft to learn how to be an effective and wise wizard. Of course, like all journeys–and like all our own lives–there are struggles... between the forces of: light and darkness, good and evil, creativity and conformity, and joy vs. rigidity and grimness.

In Harry's world, as in ours, there are two main enemies: evil and conformity. Evil is represented by men–usually it's men, isn't it?–who would like to rule everybody else. But even more abundant in our world are the ordinary people, men and women, who secretly want everybody else to be ordinary–like them. In the Harry Potter books, they are called the muggles. Harry has to spend his summer vacation with a muggles family and they are enormously threatened by Harry's magical powers. In fact, they try to keep him locked up in his room because the muggles of the world love order, tidy-ness, neatness, conformity.

43

The muggles are the enemies of joy, of magic and of the kids like Harry Potter who enjoy transforming the world, not conforming to it.

You see, there is too much about the world that needs changing, too much that is rigid, mean-spirited, boring, and limiting to the human spirit. If you conform, you just add to the rigidity, meanness, and limiting of life.

*So to be real, you have to oppose the system—and yet schools are systems which expect **con**formity. In Los Angeles, there is this big system called L.A.U.S.D.–run often by muggles who can't handle ideas that are out-of-the-box; in fact, their system is THE BOX.*

In the United States, there's an organization back east called ETS–and it is run by muggles who tell us that the worth and value of a young person can be reduced to two single numbers: an SAT verbal and an SAT math score.

And then the colleges–often run by muggles as well–take those scores and tell kids whether or not they can go to their college. Of course, they say, "We don't just use the SAT's, why, we also look at your GPA's and your AP's," but these are simply more muggle numbers.

Unfortunately, we've all been led to believe that you can measure–with a quantifiable number–what's important in education. Which is, of course, nonsense. But it is a convenient, neat way for the muggles to try to get a hold of things.

I believe, as I'm sure many of you do as well, that real education takes place in the cracks between our orderly walls and systems–for between these cracks the creative spirits escape and students are allowed to think original thoughts, explore new questions that the muggles would never dream of asking. In those less explored cracks, we can create new ways of seeing and doing.

While our society is hell bent on imposing rigid standards upon everyone pushing test scores as the only way to measure success, while all this has been going on, Crossroads School and New Roads School came into being with a radically different vision of what's important. We say it is diversity, community, caring for one another, social justice, being dedicated to saving the earth–this is what is truly important. We say diversity is what makes life exciting, but the muggles like everyone to be the same–same ideas, same skin color, same life style.

New Roads School was born five years ago, created by a bunch of anti-muggles people. That spirit is alive in the school today, but as the school becomes more and more successful, it will come under attack from the muggles of society.

So, all of you young graduates, you need to be vigilant; you need to fight for the rights of the Harry Potters to be themselves; you need to find and create the cracks in whatever systems threaten your creativity; and you need to find your own sources of joy and then "go for it."

Most of all, you need to keep the fire to the heels of the school to keep New Roads a school for wizards and not for muggles. It won't be an easy fight because the forces of darkness, the ETS folks, the test-score lackeys, the put-you-in-a-box and keep you there folks, will do everything they can to reduce joy to neatness and order.

New Roads wants to help you find magic in your education, and you must insist on that magic.

Paul F. Cummins

CUTE RULES AND GOLDEN RULES

One of the by-products of the internet and email are these cutesy and annoying "words of wisdom" that appear day after day. Recently, for example, I have had three people send me the same list of "Eleven Rules Students Do Not Learn in High School or College" which are alleged to have been laid down by Bill Gates. They are "rules" you might expect from a billionaire and the kind of tough-guy rules that macho, conservative, self-styled, rugged individualists like to pass back and forth in self-congratulatory, "Gee, aren't I clever and powerful" sessions.

To respond to all eleven rules would take more ink than the <u>Mirror</u> allows me, but I think an examination of three or four will give you an idea of their flavor. I will also offer my own annotations to these "rules."

Rule #1 - Life is not fair; get used to it. True, but it's pretty easy to get used to it if you are one of the top 1% who controls 48% of the world's wealth. Bill Gates, for example, is one of the 222 individuals whose combined wealth is equal to that of *half* the world's population! However, if you are dirt poor, watching your child die of starvation–as 20,000 children do per day–then "get used to it" isn't a really helpful attitude. It's surely not the attitude I want to teach at my schools. I would prefer: *Life is not fair; let's exert all the effort possible to make it more fair.* "Get used to it" is the position of the "haves" who are really saying, "Let's leave things the way they are: let me keep **all** my wealth and let me acquire more and more and to hell with those who have the misfortune to be born in abject poverty." Let's look at another "rule."

Rule #3 - You will <u>not</u> make 40 thousand dollars a year right out of high school. You won't be a vice president with a car phone, until you earn both. I can just hear the country club set reading rule #3 and harumphing and nodding, yes, yes, in self-righteous agreement. Opportunity is a wonderful thing, particularly when you inherit opportunity. Doonesbury (Gary Trudeau) has a wonderful cartoon (Sunday, July 2, 2000) in which an interviewer points out to George W. Bush that he was admitted to Harvard and Yale–two of the most selective universities in America–with dismal grades, that he was allowed to skip the waiting list to the National Guard, and that bankers provided him with ownership of a ball club. Clearly, opportunity for George W. Bush did not come from either achievement or flipping burgers. There are always a few people who make it out of poverty and miserable histories to become successful, but they are not the norm, and flipping burgers does not lead to Yale the way privilege does.

While most young people will not make $40,000 a year right out of high school, some do and many who have the privilege and opportunity to go to college and graduate schools will receive starting salaries over $100,000.

Recently, a friend of mine–a 14-year veteran teacher earning $39,000–received a call from his 3rd year law-school daughter. She was offered a $90,000 starting salary, asked for 2 weeks to think it over, and so the firm upped the offer to $120,000. She had good grades, so I guess you could argue that she deserved her starting salary, but did she really earn it? Or was she fortunate to be born middle-class and have the opportunity to receive a good education and go to college? The 20-25% of children born into poverty in the United States will rarely have this opportunity. Next "rule."

Rule #11 - Be nice to nerds. Chances are you'll end up working for one. Cute. It reminds me of a particularly disgusting football cheer Stanford and Northwestern students would often chant when they had losing seasons and were getting clobbered by an Arizona State or Ohio State. The cheering section would yell: "Hey, hey, that's ok, you'll be working for us someday." In other words, we may be losing this game, but we're clearly white-collar types and you–our opponents–are beneath us. I think a better rule than Rule #11 has already been formulated by virtually every religion in the world; it's the Golden Rule, the *do unto others* rule. You are nice to other people not because they may be your employers someday, but because it's the best way to live life.

In fact, when you look at the entire eleven rules, they almost all have a materialistic bent to them. The rules are all about jobs and making money, about tenure and status. Also, self-esteem is trashed. I must say I find it peculiar how often conservatives find it necessary to attack self-esteem. For example, rule #2 says that *"The world won't care about your self-esteem. The world will expect you to accomplish something **before** you feel good about yourself."* This is probably true. The world won't reward you for feeling good about yourself and achievement is a good way to gain self-esteem. However, there's no need to denigrate self-esteem while promoting achievement. It's perfectly fine to be a decent human being and feel good about that before, during, or after you accomplish anything. Again, the "new rule" #3 limits accomplishments to measurable achievements, presumably salary, wealth, stocks, status, etc. However, being a kind person, not wealthy necessarily, but kind, *is* an accomplishment.

So, please folks, don't send me another set of the eleven rules, or any other precious bits of Babbitry. Send me a superb poem or some real wisdom–not heated up Calvin Coolidge-isms.

Paul F. Cummins

ARTS AND ADVOCATES

Often we hear that so and so is an arts advocate, or that such and such is an arts advocacy organization. Why is it, we ought to wonder, that the arts so often need advocates? In other nations the value of the arts is clear to all. Many nations have adequate funding for the arts (we do *not* in America) and in many lands the arts are so organic to the health and well being of all people that they need no advocates–they simply are a deep part of life itself.

I would like to play my role as an arts advocate by offering some arguments as to why the arts are so crucial for children and society. For those who like lists, here are twelve arguments for the arts–the first six are courtesy of William Cleveland (another arts advocate); the last six are my own.

1. The arts help us communicate about transcendent values and issues: Indeed, the arts speak to levels of human consciousness in unique ways which only they can reach. Without the arts in our curriculum, we deprive children of a deep human need, the need to explore mystery;

2. The arts are a basic educational reform: There are many different kinds of intelligences, and the arts offer an alternative for success and respectability for students who may not do as well in other subjects;

3. The arts provide a common language in a complex global culture: The arts build bridges between radically different cultures and languages groups;

4. The arts help maintain our competitiveness in a technological age: Artists are innovators. "The roles of the artist and the technological innovator are often interchangeable. In his book, *The Paradox of the Silicon Savior*, Grant Venerable points out "that the very best engineers and technical designers (in the Silicon Valley) are, nearly without exception, practicing musicians";

5. The arts are a proven strategy for healing, prevention and empowerment: This assertion is almost self-explanatory. In case study after study, Venerable continues, the arts are shown "to be an effective and cost-beneficial resource for reducing violence, recidivism, and psychopathology;"

6. The arts are an essential resource for community development: they provide jobs, encourage tourism, attract audiences. "Recent research shows that each dollar spent on the arts generates three to four dollars in non-arts expenditures."

To Cleveland's list of six, I would add a few others:

7. Programs in the arts can radically improve graduation rates, grades, and overall achievement levels: This has been demonstrated in report after study after conference (*U.S. News and World Report*, March 30, 1992);

8. The arts teach skills needed in the twenty-first century work force: The capacity for working in teams, creative thinking, self-esteem, imagination, invention. All are the province of the arts;

9. The arts develop leadership: In every artistic endeavor the best artists are pushing the boundaries of human knowledge, expanding the breadth and understanding of human experience, and creating for the world something that was not there before. We bemoan our lack of leadership in politics and education today and yet we cut from the curriculum this important arena for developing leaders. It makes no sense.

10. The arts inspire self-confidence and help keep kids interested in school: My own experience has shown that often a recorder class or a painting class is *the* class that keeps a student coming to school instead of dropping out and then becoming an "at-risk" student, some of whom inevitably join the prison culture rather than the culture-at-large;

11. The arts help energize the school environment: Paintings in the halls, murals on the walls, music assemblies, recorder and song at ceremonies, plays and dance recitals–all breathe life into a school. In the past few years, I have watched the arts lift the morale of several entire schools–principals, teachers, parents, as well as students;

12. The arts are a crucial way to honor and celebrate the earth: If we accept the argument of Thomas Berry and Miriam McGillis that our main purpose as humans is to celebrate our emergence as the beings in which the earth becomes conscious of itself, then the arts are the *primary* means by which we celebrate this process.

To conclude this article on the power of the arts let's take a look at two quotes: one from Ernest Fleishmann, former Executive Vice President and Managing Director of the Los Angeles Philharmonic, and the other from author Katherine Ann Porter.

> History does not measure a nation's greatness by its corporate balance sheets, or even by its military bands. It is to the writers, the

musicians, the philosophers, the painters and sculptors, the builders of the great cathedrals that we look for inspiration, for the impetus to create and go forward to make a positive impact on the world's civilization. If, however, we follow the dictates of the anti-arts brigade in Congress, the impact of the United States on the cultural progress of our world will be one of shame and sorrow, of guns and jails, and bottom lines.

-Ernest Fleishmann

The arts live continuously, and they live literally by faith; their nature and their shapes and their uses survive unchanged in all that matters through times of interruption, diminishment, neglect; they outlive governments and creeds and societies, even the very civilizations that produced them. They cannot be destroyed altogether because they represent the substance of faith and the only reality. They are what we find again when the ruins are cleared away.

-Katherine Ann Porter

AFFIRMATIVE ACTION, RACISM, AND PROGRESS: THE ROLE OF EDUCATION

Until we become a color-blind and an equitable society, we will need to provide programs such as welfare and affirmative action (not affirmative access) to provide a more level playing field. Unfortunately, pseudo-science mixed with incendiary ideology has had a profound impact on our thinking. Similar to "welfare," somehow the term "affirmative action" picked up all sorts of negative trappings on its travels. As it became a conservative conclusion that welfare "hasn't worked," politicians and critics of varying political stripes began announcing that affirmative action hasn't worked either. Even a Supreme Court justice who was a product of affirmative action began to trash the term once he achieved success.

In point of fact, welfare has worked for millions of people; it just hasn't solved all our social problems which, of course, it was never intended to do. It was to be a lifeline for those cast adrift and drowning. Solutions for unemployment, poverty, and educational inequities need to come from elsewhere–they are not the province of welfare.

The decisions to eliminate "welfare as we know it" have both figuratively and literally thrown many babies out with the bath water. Meanwhile, affirmative action at its best enabled many to make substantial gains. In fact, William G. Bowen, a former President of Princeton University, and Derek Bok, a former President of Harvard University, have in their recent (1998) book, *The Shape Of The River* demonstrated that "race-sensitive admissions policies in American colleges and universities have worked very well in accomplishing the objectives they were instituted to achieve: (a) educating increasing numbers of minority graduates who would enter the professions and assume positions of civic and community leadership within a population that will soon be one-third (1/3) black and Hispanic; and (b) creating a racially diverse educational environment to help all their students learn to live and work successfully in an increasingly multi-racial society."

However, in the current backlash mood, these gains are minimized and the crises of a James Bakke or a Cheryl Hopwood become the "cause celebres" of the white power structure and hence, of course, of the press.

Clearly, the Bakke decision (1978) and Hopwood v Texas (1996) have raised enormously complicated issues and questions. But, for the foreseeable future, it *is* clear that "the consequence of a purely class-based (non-color based) affirmative action policy would be virtually all-white colleges and law schools" (Jeffrey Rosen, *The New Republic*, Oct. 17, 1994). It is also clear that racial preferences would need to persist for a long time to achieve any kind of reasonable representation of blacks and Mexican Americans in colleges and graduate schools. Why? Because, as Roger Wilkens wrote, you cannot expect rapid progress from an entire group of people who, for example, "have been on this North American continent for 375 years and that, for 245, the country permitted slavery... and that for the next hundred years [we] had legalized subordination of blacks, under a suffocating blanket of condescension and frequently enforced by night-riding terrorists. We've had only thirty years of something else."

The achievement of a color-blind society is a worthwhile dream, but a dream that is unlikely to be realized even in the 21st century. Skin color will very likely continue to be the predominant factor in categorizing people. Only when people of varying skin colors and other so-called racial characteristics are accorded truly equal educational and economic opportunities will these superficial differences begin to melt away. Thus, whether we call it affirmative action or some other more neutral term, we must address the class/race inequities which haunt this country and that hang as a curse over everyone's head.

To live in a world where cultural differences are honored and acknowledged, but are not the defining and delimiting characteristics of relationships—is this possible? Not as long as we continue to stereotype and debase groups of people according to the dictates of pseudo-science, bigotry, and ignorance.

Perhaps, however, we can unlearn our prejudices by going back to the very beginning of our species. When we study our origins, we find that we humans are closely related to chimpanzees and that our racial codifications are not only un-scientific, but often silly. Given the numerous ways of chemically and genetically classifying humans, we see that skin color is a relatively minor and even misleading method of differentiating groups of people. Other means range from susceptibility to malaria, or the presence or absence of the enzyme lactose to body shapes—tall, short, wide or narrow buttocks to the amount of body hair or color of the nipples—and the list goes on. As Jared Diamond points out, "There is a third possible explanation for the function of geographically variable human traits, besides survival or sexual selection; namely no function at all... If we classify human populations by their fingerprints, most Europeans and black Africans would sort out into one race, Jews and some Indonesians into another, and aboriginal Australians in still another" (*Discovery Magazine*, Nov. 1994).

What we can learn from this all is the idiocy of classifying each other for hierarchic purposes and subjugating or killing each other according to one codification or another. Prejudice is a learned behavior, and it can be *un*learned through education. Better yet, it can be shunned in the first place so that it need not be corrected at a later date. Bigotry is one of the most ugly and degrading forms of human behavior; it drags down perpetrator and recipient alike. There is hope, however, for racism is based primarily upon fear and ignorance. It is the enemy of good education, and educators can use racism as a means of discussing ways in which humanity can reach light rather than perpetuating darkness. Clearly the goal of transcending this curse upon humanity needs to be a primary focus of all peoples and all schools. Our well-being as a species depends upon this "new education."

POLITICS AND SOCIETY

PRIORITIES

Priorities, priorities, priorities. It all comes down to priorities, doesn't it? The stock market has hit 11,000 several times recently and fortunes are being made daily. The number of millionaires is swelling and even billionaires are on the rise.

But wait, there's a problem we just don't want to acknowledge. Things aren't that great for some 30 to 36 million Americans (14 million of whom are children). What's their problem? They are hungry. A 1996 report from the Tufts University Center On Hunger, Poverty, and Nutrition Policy informs us that the number of poorly fed Americans rose from 20 million to 30 million between 1985 and 1990–an increase of 50 percent! Furthermore, a 1996 U.S. Department of Agriculture report states that the number has actually risen to 36 million–including 14 million children. How could this be? Priorities. Priorities.

First of all, the priorities of the media are to make a profit and to serve their bosses–those who are benefitting from the current economic boom. Thus, the media does not feature "hunger amidst plenty" stories because: 1) hunger doesn't sell the way Monica Lewinsky or O.J. or Gary Condit "sells" and, 2) "hunger amidst plenty" might suggest that a redistribution of wealth, resources, and opportunity might be called for, and this might fuel the fires for change, and those who are doing very well, thank you very much, don't want change.

Second, according to Peter Rosset of the Food First Organization, "In America, people go hungry because they cannot afford both food and housing." Notice we are not talking only about people on welfare; we are talking about people who work, but still can't afford both food and shelter. Doesn't this suggest that salaries, benefits, and hourly wages need major adjustments?

Third, we need to remind ourselves that, in fact, there is enough food to go around. According to numerous national and international organizations, both in the USA and in the entire world, there is enough food to feed every man, woman, and child. As Food First states, "The real culprits are an economy that fails to offer everyone opportunities and a society that places economic efficiency over compassion."

Fourth, while population size is perhaps the major threat to the world's well-being, it is not currently the main reason why people go hungry. The main reason is that, as a 1999 U.N. Human Development report says, "Global inequities in income and living standards have reached grotesque proportions." One such factor in our living standards is our devotion to eating meat. Currently, enormous earth resources go to feeding the animals we slaughter for meat. "Much of our planet's crops do not go to feed people at all–they are fed to livestock," argues Douglas H. Boucher in "The Paradox of Plenty: Hunger in a

Bountiful World" (Food First, 1999). This is not to say that population size doesn't contribute to hunger.

Also, the living standards dictated by men around the planet have placed women in a subservient role, and this combined with poverty in general leads to overpopulation. As a recent article in *The Progressive* (Dec. 1999) reminds us, "When women have an adequate income, a decent education, and political freedom, they have fewer and fewer babies." Simply stated, fewer people means less food required to feed us all.

We need to see that hunger is really a function of our democracy not working well. Hunger will disappear only when democracy operates efficiently. Senator Bill Bradley proposed that we reduce by half the number of children living below the poverty line. Priorities again. Cut children living in poverty by half, yet maintain our bloated military budget–to defend ourselves again whom? Let half of American's hunger driven children stay hungry, while we fatten the military coffers? Bradley would have allocated $10 billion annually to feed half of our nation's hungry children. The Pentagon's budget is $270 billion annually. What's wrong with this picture? Priorities.

EMBARRASSING, I.E., INTELLECTUALLY UNCOUTH QUESTIONS

There are certain questions which rarely get asked. And, since rarely asked, they receive little discourse. They are embarrassing to us all. To ask them means you might get an answer–and the answer might be reasonable. And, therefore, some *action* might reasonably be expected, or even seem compelling. So better not to ask the questions at all. Certainly these are questions you won't hear discussed in the major media outlets.

"Oh, go ahead," someone says. "Go ahead. Nobody will pay much attention anyhow. We're all so inundated with mind-numbing and dumbing 'news' reports, analyses, talk-shows, etc., that any questions of any real significance will simply get glossed over, slopped over, or buried... so go ahead." "Okay, then, here are a few questions."

1. Why do we, as the richest nation in the history of the world, accept and allow homelessness and child poverty?

2. Why do we believe that being the gun capital and homicide capital of the planet makes us "safe"?

3. Why do we accept the purchase of political offices with funding of over 70% for both parties funds provided by special interests, lobbies, and corporate America?

4. What is the purpose of a cold-war-proportioned military budget, now that the Cold War has ended and, as William Greider writes, Our only serious adversary has evaporated into history?

5. Why did we become so outraged by the forced evacuations of the Kosovars but continue to ignore and violate treaties with the Native Americans our nation dispossessed?

6. Why have we allowed the ratio of CEO income to worker income to become wider and wider (the most extreme in the world) with no end in sight and with not so much as a whisper of protest?

7. Why are we willing to spend more on building new prisons than new schools?

8. When we fight vicious terrorists and nasty foreign leaders, where have they acquired their guns and weapons?

9. Who is the biggest manufacturer, exporter, and profiteer of guns and ammunition on the planet?

10. Why are we willing to base so much of our consumer comfort on the pitiful and obscene wages of Third World workers and child laborers?

Just some idle questions. I don't propose to have answers for these questions, although some of the answers are virtually embodied in the questions themselves. For example, we don't need to tolerate child poverty, homelessness, "purchased" elections, guns on the streets, etc. We have the funds to eliminate them all. What we lack is citizen interest and political leadership. The least we can do is to ask some difficult questions.

Why is it then that the media generally avoids these questions? Well, if you take a Chomsky-ish position–dismissed usually as paranoid-left-wing-extremism–then you might posit the following: the function of the media is to distract us from serious issues. By serious, I mean issues that might threaten the power structure of society as it is currently constituted. As it is, a few people, a few corporations wield inordinate power. They own the media. They hire the media pundits, and the pundits know their role: to entertain, to seem to discuss issues deeply but never to challenge the basic premises of our society which dictate that the rich stay rich (and get richer and richer), that the poor stay poor (after all, for the poor not to be poor would require some redistribution of wealth), and that the general public be convinced that ours is the best of all possible systems.

Of course, the government seems to be a key partner in all this. It, too, will not raise any of the above ten questions in any significant way. For it too is the "employee" of the real power brokers and corporate forces. Its function is to see that no significant legislation is ever passed that might redistribute power in any way other than the way it is.

Consequently, the government will give lip service to the needs of the poor, the need to rebuild inner cities and the needs of all citizens for adequate education and health care. Nonetheless, our legislators will not seek the tax revenues required to enact legislation which could address these problems. In fact, rather than raise taxes, since the "Reagan Revolution" the government has lowered income taxes, corporate taxes, capital gains taxes, and inheritance taxes. Rather than redistribute wealth, the government has seen to it that the wealthy keep more and more of their wealth as the disparity between rich and poor grows wider and wider.

In reality, the Congress and the President were hired by the power brokers *not* to significantly change anything. Certainly they will not change the absurd way that we have structured elections to go to the highest bidder. The elected officials know to whom they are beholden and it is not the ordinary voter or citizen.

And why is there so little public outrage, anger, or active efforts to change things? Perhaps because the public has not only been lulled into media-induced stupor, but also because there is an overall sense of hopelessness, a sense that the government is not responsive to real needs and that our politicians are bought, not very bright, and sometimes even corrupt.

So, forget those difficult questions; let's flip on the television and see what's the latest scandal or piece of gossip.

Paul F. Cummins

TIME IS RUNNING OUT

In 1982, Jonathan Schell wrote a book, <u>The Fate of the Earth</u>, which may be regarded someday as a critical event in the preservation of the planet. In 1982, the Cold War was still intense. "I'd rather be dead than red," was a mentality–if you could call it such–that still shaped both foreign policy and public attitudes. This mentality led us to establish a nuclear system for killing 200 to 400 million Russians should they cross a forbidden border. All of this was to be done in the name of freedom. Say what?

In 1982, both Russia and the United States had thousands of nuclear warheads poised, targeted, and ready to be sent off to mutually destroy each other and perhaps all human life. Enter Jonathan Schell.

Jonathan Schell, along with a few other lonesome voices including Helen Caldicott, Bertrand Russell, and Albert Einstein, was one of the first writers to devote a full length study of the immediate danger of the human race rendering itself extinct. <u>The Fate of the Earth</u>, which first appeared in 1981 in three separate issues of *The New Yorker*, was a crucial ground-breaking, consciousness-raising account of the nuclear crisis. Schell described the insanity of the arms race, the hideous redundancy of the U.S. and Russian arsenals of nuclear weapons, and the distinct possibility that the world might come to an end.

In a second book two years later, <u>The Abolition</u> (1984), Schell wrote:

> For the risk of extinction is not just one more item on the agenda of issues that faces us. Embracing, as it does, the life and death of every human being on earth and every future human being, it embraces and transcends all other issues.

Facing this issue Schell then, and now again, proposes the only sane and the only real possible solution for mankind–the abolition of nuclear weapons. As Albert Einstein wrote in 1946, "As history has proven conclusively, preparation for war always leads to actual war."

Schell was one of the first who had the courage and wisdom to counter-act the needless jingoism that was essentially operating on its own momentum with no public debate. Schell also pointed out that we humans were taking a billions-of-years process of national evolution out of the forces of nature and putting the future of the planet in the hands of immature frail human actors:

> Thought and will now became mightier than the earth that had given birth to them. Now human beings became actors in the geological time

span, and the laws that had governed the development and the survival of life began to be superseded by processes in the mind of man.

We humans, as Schell pointed out, took evolution off automatic pilot and put it on manual, with a few ideologically obsessed men sitting at hair-trigger control of weapons of cosmic destructiveness. It was–and still is–a terrible, terrible situation. And no one was talking about it! That's when Jonathan Schell entered the picture the first time (in 1981/82.)

Now, at the end of the 20th century, with the potential of new millennium thinking at hand, enter, again, Jonathan Schell. In 1998, Schell published The Gift of Time, proclaiming that we have a historical moment in time when it is possible to rid the world of nuclear weapons–a moment which may never come again. In The Gift of Time, Schell interviews leading figures of the cold was and finds support for complete nuclear disarmament. For example, former Allied Arm Forces Commander in the Gulf War, Charles Horner, states, "If you own them [nuclear weapons], you legitimize them just by your ownership."

Well, we certainly legitimize them in the U.S. Even though the Cold War is over, we possess 10,000 nuclear weapons and we spend over $35 billion annually developing and maintaining nuclear weapons. In fact, we have spend over 5.5 trillion (in 1996 dollars) on nuclear weapons since 1940–more than Medicare and Social Security combined. Clearly, it is time to rid the planet of the cancerous growths of nuclear arms.

But is abolition possible? Some would argue no. Schell responds by saying that if we need only to get the U.S., Russia, China, France, England, India, Pakistan, and Israel to agree, then it doesn't seem completely out of the question. The gift of time that we have is to work hard now–with only eight nations to bring together. But with Iran, Iraq, and North Korea on the verge of nuclear ownership, and who knows how many more in the near future, the time to act is now.

It does not take too much imagination to foresee the dangers of accidental ignition of a nuclear war or future use by ideological maniacs. Furthermore, the possibilities of both the miniaturization of atomic power and, therefore, the widespread blackmail potential and use by terrorist organizations ought to be enough to compel immediate control of nuclear materials while we still have time: *the gift of time.*

Unfortunately, the U.S. policies currently are timid isolationist, and still reflective of cold war thinking. Charles Horner remarks, "It's amazing how many people cannot envision a world free of nuclear weapons." To my way of thinking, this gift of time is one offered primarily to the U.S. The U.S. possesses almost 50% of the world's strategic nuclear warheads. Consequently, there is a major question on the U.S. table: Shall we lead the entire world to safety and sanity; or do we continue to require a huge advantage over the entire world thus requiring them to seek more arms to protect themselves? The answer ought to be obvious to all thinking human beings. But clearly it is not. Enter Jonathan Schell.

In his conclusion to The Gift of Time [a book I urge all Americans to read], Schell offers us a challenge we can ill afford to ignore:

> Once, the arrival in the world of new generations took care of itself. Now, they can come into existence only if, through an act of faith and collective will, we ensure their right to exist. Performing that act is the greatest of responsibilities of the generations now alive. The gift of time is the gift of life, forever, if we know how to receive it.

NOTE: This article was written before the recent decision by the U.S. Senate to refuse to sign the Nuclear Arms Test Ban Treaty. A shameful decision, in the opinion of this author.

FURTHER NOTE: Jonathan Schell won a 1999 Lannan Foundation Award for writing.

AN ARMS RACE WITH OURSELVES

Because it's night and the barbarians haven't come.
And some people just in from the border say
There are no barbarians any longer.
Now what's going to happen to us without them?
The barbarians were a kind of solution.

–C. P. Cavafy

Guns do not make people safe. Clearly, humanity was safer before men invented and began the relentless proliferation and intensification of guns and their range and power. Certainly we in America are *less* safe having more guns out on the street than there are in any other country. Proof: more Americans per capita and in total die of gun shots than in any other country! But such is our (neurosis? idiocy? insanity?) condition that we have now imposed this same twisted logic onto the global defense scene.

A little background: In the 1930s we were mired down in a depression. World War II mobilized our citizens and our economy and ever since we have been dependent–in varying degrees–upon a war time mentality and productivity. No sooner did we defeat fascism in Germany and Japan than a new enemy emerged–communism in Russia–or so we convinced ourselves. Thus began the infamous arms race that engendered a nuclear nightmare for all of humanity. Then in 1989 the Soviet Union unraveled. A "peace dividend" was promised for America and the world. However, it hasn't happened. Why? Because in truth we have become dependent on a war-time economy. As we mobilized for World War II, we created what Dwight Eisenhower referred to as the "military-industrial complex." Actually, in his farewell address, Ike warned the country against this marriage. More recent critics have referred to this complex as the "iron triangle" of Congress, the defense companies, and the Pentagon. Thus, the Cold War (1948-1989 and its successor 'the new world order') has been a five-decade period of such profits and mobilization for the M-I Complex that we seem to now believe it is a necessity of economic life. Defense now has its own momentum and keeps rolling along even though there is really no one against whom we are defending ourselves.

Although few politicians would admit it, we are now rather at sea without the Russian bogey man to justify our arms build up. Now that the bogey man is gone, what pray tell is the justification for continuing our bloated defense spending? (Currently it is larger today in constant dollars than it was in the mid-70s, the peak of the cold war.) We try to pretend that we need our current massive capacity for over-kill because of "terrorists" but even though the press obediently promulgates this government line, it is difficult to believe. We continue to build more tanks, more bombers, more this, more that, but who is our so mighty enemy? Hussein? Arafat? And, as if this were not reason enough to pause and reconsider our bondage to defense spending, there is another even more compelling reason: we are making the entire planet less and less safe by arming others.

Before discussing the arming of others, there is one other factor to consider. Despite its momentum and high levels of spending, all is not well in the defense industry. Because of the glut of planes, tanks, and other items, and because newer models are increasingly sophisticated and costly, the actual number of orders from the U.S. military is down. For example, in the 1980s Fort Worth was turning out nearly 300 F-16s annually; now it is making only eighty or so a year. And, as William Greider points out (in his recent study, <u>Fortress America</u>), "almost none of those 80 planes are for defending America!" So, rather than re-access the rationale for continuing old modes of defense, we seek to keep our arms industry alive by exporting arms to other nations. The system is really rather absurd: we build F-16s, we sell them to other nations, we then say since other nations have F-16s we must build F-22s. This is all fine and good for defense contractors, but the tax payers are footing the bill. The tragedy of it all is that every dollar spent on defense is a dollar denied to education, health, the infrastructure, national parks and ecosystems. Congress is unwilling to offend its defense buddies and supporters and so, even though orders in the U.S. are down, the defense companies sell their weapons abroad.

Countries around the world are being armed by the U.S. and the U.S. then determines to play world policeman. Defense spending, for example, is up by 35% in Latin American countries since 1992. Their economies are only up by 22%. While it may be good business to sell weapons, it is making the planet less and less safe for everyone.

One is struck by the blithe, unchallenged, assumption that war is inevitable, forever inevitable (otherwise why do we continue R & D for more sophisticated and devastating means of waging war?) **and** that we must pour untold billions of dollars and some of our best creative energy into imaging new wartime-techno-futuristic scenes. Further, we assume that an equivalent amount of money, time, and energy should not be put into studying, networking among nations, holding the highest level conferences to find ways of *dis*-arming and seeking the peaceful care, protection, and cleaning of our precious and fragile planet and its peoples.

As you sow, so shall you reap. If we continue to sow arms, is there any question what the harvest will be? As Greider writes, "By pushing more and more weaponry, old and new, on other nations, the arms manufacturers are laying the groundwork for future conflicts... The U.S. government spends twelve times more on promoting arms sales abroad than on environmental technologies." With the collapse of the Soviet Union, there is a unique opportunity for the world to stop the senseless intensification and proliferation of weapons in the world. The U.S. could take a leadership role in peace rather than in producing the means of war on a mass global scale. Do we wish to lead the world to peace or are the economic needs of a few so dominant that a future of truly terrifying proportions will be imposed upon humanity by the purveyors of arms? The "iron triangle" seems unwilling to stop what some refer to as the U.S.' arms race with itself. Ultimately, an enlightened and, I suspect, an indignant citizenry will be the only ones to put a stop to this madness.

Paul F. Cummins

ONLY WAY TO END GUN HOMICIDES IS TO OUTLAW ALL GUNS NOW

I am not optimistic that Congress will make any substantial changes in this country's gun control laws, because most legislators are content to let the National Rifle Association (NRA) and other gun huggers call the shot, so to say, and sit by while America fortifies its position as the homicide capital of the planet.

Every now and then, and lately with increasing frequency, a mass murder takes place that temporarily disturbs our normally gun-indifferent to gun-loving society. But most legislators know that the American public in general has the attention span of a fruit fly and they employ a stall-and-delay strategy that allows them to accomplish nothing substantive–which is their standard approach to most major issues.

The rub comes when too many gun-assisted acts of violence occur too close together and certain members of Congress, fearful of losing votes, act. Note that they act to save votes, not lives.

I suppose I sound cynical, but having watched guns proliferate in the streets all my life and seeing homicide rates grow and grow, as one Congress after another does little but repeat gun lobby slogans, ("Guns don't kill people, people do"), it's hard to be anything but cynical.

We get what we're willing to get–spineless and visionless politicians, who do the minimum in fear of offending monied interests and do that only under pressure. Shortly after the tragedy at Littleton, Colorado, the California legislature passed the most ludicrous piece of legislation I have heard of in years. Citizens can now only buy one gun per month in California. Only 12 guns a year: goodness gracious, how will we manage?

Consider these facts:

1. In 1995, there were 77 homicides with guns in England, while there were 13,673 in America.

2. 110 people die from gun fire *every day* in America.

3. Between 1979 and 1991, as many children died from gunshot wounds in America as American soldiers died in Vietnam.

4. For every attacker shot and killed in self-defense, 130 Americans are shot and killed by guns in other circumstances. 1:130. Is this safe? Is this sane?

What would I like our legislators to do? Although there isn't a remote possibility that my proposals would be seriously considered, I will outline a plan for an ideal America, in order to imagine a safe, sane, peaceful and civil society for a moment.

1. Only the police and the military shall possess guns.

2. Everyone else will turn in their guns at the nearest police station or National Guard post.

3. The government will buy these guns–at one price for the first six months and at a declining price for the next six months.

4. Ammunition will be sold only to the military and the police.

5. People committing crimes with guns will be severely punished.

In short, I propose the total elimination and abolition of guns for citizens. Is this so terribly radical? It was proposed seven years ago by Senator John Chaffee, Republican of Rhode Island.

Whenever I present my plan to listeners, two arguments inevitable emerge: one, it's our constitutional right to carry guns; two, you'll never get rid of all the guns out there.

Of course, we won't get rid of all the guns. There are 200 million guns now in circulation. But since their primary function is to kill living things, why manufacture more? The more guns there are on the street, the more people are likely to be wounded or die. So let's begin reducing the number of guns and maybe eventually we'll get rid of them. But we'll never get rid of them unless we begin.

As to the constitutional question. The Framers died 200 years ago. They were concerned about British soldiers capturing American villages and intruding into people's homes. They did not anticipate 14-year-olds slaughtering their classmates with automatic weapons.

The second amendment says, "A well-regulated militia, being necessary to the security of a free state, the right of the people to keep and bear arms, shall not be infringed."

I take this literally: it is the well-regulated militia which shall keep and bear arms, meaning the military and the police, not millions of individuals shooting each other and innocent victims and bystanders at an obscene rate. The second amendment speaks in terms of collective protection–"a well-regulated militia" and "the People"–not unregulated individuals bearing arms.

Furthermore, common sense tells us that violent acts of passion and anger, as well as robberies and murders committed with guns, will kill a lot more people than knives, clubs and fists. It's simple: if there are fewer guns, fewer innocent people will die.

As I said, I have little or no hope that our legislators will make any intelligent changes in gun laws. While safety locks, registration checks, and the inclusion of pawn shops in the customer check process may help a little, it is clear that our elected officials will find ways to water down, write in loopholes, evade and obfuscate any serious legislation. The killing in our streets and homes will continue unabated.

After all, guns and ammunition are big business and, as President Calvin Coolidge said, "the business of America is business."

PRESERVING OUR WILD HERITAGE

Spending the turn of the century in the Galápagos was indeed a fortunate opportunity for my wife, our friends and me. We spent the beginning of the 21st century looking back into pre-historic time. On our third day, we visited the oldest of the islands, Española, which dates back over three million years. The island is populated with a dazzling contingent of birds: blue footed boobies, masked boobies, albatrosses, turtles (sea and land), sea lions, marine iguanas, and more. We felt extraordinarily blessed to be snorkeling with the huge turtles, as well as the playful sea lion pups nearby, and mingling with exotic fish and rays; we were reminded of how precious the remaining wild life habitats are to our individual and collective souls. Sitting upon the warm white sands with sea lion pups cavorting and nursing within several feet, with the gorgeous pelicans slicing the water in their amazing dives, with the frigate birds performing breathtaking aerial maneuvers, and with the giant sea turtles bobbing and gliding by, brought us in touch with what is truly valuable. Not the acquisition of things and property, but the life force. The life force originates from creativity and thrives on diversity.

In the 19th century, the poet Wordsworth wrote that "getting and spending, we lay waste our powers." However, today, we lay waste not only to ourselves, but we lay waste to the Earth itself. I like to think that if every human who dwells on the planet could sit for just a half hour a week with wild creatures, he or she would become a fierce advocate for preserving their habitats. After a time, each of us would come to see that there is only one habitat–Earth. Cities with pavement and smog and high-rise dwellings are a distortion of life. Worse, they are the result of our crazy customs, certain religious doctrines, and mindless practices have led to the human over-population and resource deprivation of the planet. We have taken nature off of automatic pilot and put her on manual–with us recklessly at the controls. Consequently, our technology allows us to over-populate without natural selection processes to hold our numbers down. I would not, for a minute, argue that we should simply allow natural forces to hold down our numbers, however, careful planning would do so, that is, if certain religious dogmas were not in place. Thus, too many people, rampant technology, and unrestrained avarice lead to the on-going destruction of our common habitat. We are so immersed in the forest we cannot see the beauty of the trees. And then, quite literally, we chop down the trees. Each time we lose a piece of this or that wildlife habitat, we diminish our own heritage, our children's heritage, and, consequently, we diminish our own souls. For when you have no wild-*ness*, wilderness, to communicate with, a piece of your own self remains mute and, what's more, may never recognize that you have lost anything.

71

The Galápagos are under assault–the Ecuadorian economy is so messed up that tourist dollars are eagerly sought and more and more people (myself among them) visit the islands each year, with the inevitable chipping away of their pristine conditions. I know I have offered a contradiction, for if we can't visit the wild places, how can we nurture this communication that I state is so important? There is no simple answer. However, I believe tourism is a lesser evil. The greater evil is the world wide elimination of resources and species all in the name of quick profit. Profiteers almost wiped out completely and forever the great tortoises of the Galápagos. Thousands of other species across the Earth have, in fact, been totally wiped out. And thousands of other species, including the magnificent elephants of Africa, are now critically endangered. What can each of us do to save the wild creatures and all the interdependent features of the Earth? What can we do?

Well, perhaps we can express our rage and demand that our elected officials put this issue at the top of their lists. The Bible asks, "What shall it profit a man to gain the world and lose his soul?" How about this rephrase: What shall it gain a man/woman to lose the land and its wildness and to lose his/her soul as well? The greatest blessing the earth has to offer is the Earth's very diversity of living creatures. We are only one species among thousands. It is our arrogance and ignorance that places greed above the preservation of our fellow inhabitants. Their continued future is inextricably bound with our own. This simple realization is a necessary first step. Theoretically, I know this to be true. Visiting the Galápagos and watching the golden iguana eating a cactus flower, or a majestic albatross take off and glide over the sea, was a glorious reminder. These reminders are critical to our own survival and our own relationship to the Earth.

TROUBLE IN PARADISE

Over the winter break (1999-2000) my wife and I spent a week in paradise and then a week amidst the wonders of the Galapagos. Paradise describes the beautiful Hacienda Cusin ninety minutes north of Quito, Ecuador. The Dueno is a remarkable man, a British emigrant and former prep school teacher from New York, Nicholas T. Millhouse. The Hacienda will accommodate up to 40 guests and the grounds are absolutely astonishing. (Anyone interested in learning about his accommodations can email him at: hacienda@cusin.com.ec)

While I enjoyed my rest, reading, relaxation, and short excursions for sampling the local culture and history, it was difficult to avert my eyes from the ubiquitous and overwhelming poverty surrounding the Hacienda and permeating the entire country. From our first arrival, at 10:30 p.m., we were besieged by children four to ten years old begging in the airport parking area where our van awaited. And in the central plaza near our Hacienda, at every turn of the market, I encountered tiny, toothless old women, their bodies bent over from decades of hard labor, with no means of support other than begging. The children have little hope other than to scratch out a living farming, begging, finding menial part-time work; their limited education–poor at that–ended in 4th grade.

When we arrived (December 26), the Ecuador sucre was pegged at 18,500 to one dollar. During the next week, it went up to as high as 29,000 and, when we left, it was frozen at 25,000. This is, of course, particularly disastrous to small business people who borrow against dollars and then have to pay back their loans with sucres of less value.

I had never paid much attention to Ecuador; however, I learned that things there are much the same as other parts of the globe. The very rich are very rich and are becoming more so; the very poor remain very poor. The government is fragmented (there are 15 political parties vying for power), often corrupt, and utterly beholden to the very rich. Often, through their corruption, government leaders themselves become rich. Occasionally they become too greedy and bungle their efforts to loot the national coffers and, like Abdala `El Loco' Bucaram, are run out of the country–though often taking enough wealth with them to live luxuriously elsewhere. The army exists to protect the social hierarchy, though periodically an army commander will try to grab the government for himself. Local police are often inept, corrupt, and unreliable. So, it's pretty clear to see why the poor remain poor. Who is there to speak out for them, to lobby for their rights, to provide leadership and seek reform?

One day, one of our travel companions, a fellow educator, went for a long hike and got a little lost. Walking up a long trail he came to what he thought was a public hacienda. It was, instead, the private estate of an absurdly wealthy young Ecuadorian who inherited his vast wealth, had a completely condescending view of the poor, and told my friend that Ecuador would benefit under a dictator who should exterminate about 50,000 or so undesirables, which he implied meant campesinos or indigenous, or as tourists might call them, Indians. And, of course, it is the indigenous who seem to be the victims year after year, century after century. They toil and work the land so that others may profit.

It is difficult to see how this pattern of government corruption, economic exploitation, and appalling discrepancies of wealth, can be broken in Ecuador, or anywhere else for that matter. Education is certainly one answer. However, there must also be genuine leadership emanating from the higher powers. It would be a wonderful, new, albeit radical approach for the U.S.A. to support populist leaders, reformers, and true progressives in foreign countries instead of the support we throw to various dictators by whom invariably are later embarrassed, have to renounce, or quietly disown (i.e., Ngo Dinh Diem, Manuel Noriega, Saddam Hussein, Prince Sihanouk, Pinochet, Bin Laden, et al.), and other such autocrats who receive U.S. aid. One has to admit, a stunning array of mass murderers, psychopaths, and egomaniacs we often choose to support. But here's a new idea: Why don't we provide aid to the people who suffer rather than the exploiters? Well, it's a new century and it doesn't do any harm to dream a little...

IF WOMEN RULED THE WORLD

A few years ago I stumbled upon a quote of Gabriel Garcia Marquez which I found stunning, a quote that rings true and which may even come true someday. Perhaps the 21st century will move history a step closer towards its realization. Without any further delay, here is the quote:

> The only new idea that could save humanity in the twenty-first century is for women to take over the management of the world. I believe that male hegemony has squandered opportunity of 10,000 years. We men have belittled and ridiculed feminine intuition, and on the other hand, we have historically sanctified our ideologies, almost all of them absurd or abominable. The masculine power structure has proved that it cannot impede the destruction of the environment because it is incapable of overcoming its own interests. For women, on the other hand, the preservation of the environment is a genetic vocation. The reversal of powers is a matter of life and death.

It is hard to imagine how men could have messed up the planet any more than they have done to date. They (we) seem incapable of living in peace with each other. Whenever any peoples anywhere organize into a grouping or society of any kind, two things happen: 1) men use their physical might to assume absolute dominance over everyone else in the group, and 2) they wage wars against any other grouping that is nearby and that doesn't share their exact beliefs and behavior. Perhaps if women assumed leadership of their respective societies, men would have to find more constructive activities than to spend billions of dollars inventing and utilizing weapons and other means of destruction and environmental exploitation. Men seem to define progress in terms of how fast they can do things; speed is of the essence to men. Kill more, faster; deplete environmental resources more, faster. Perhaps having had the perspective of observing male stupidity, cupidity, and rapacity for several millennia, women might develop a more intelligent and less self-destructive way of organizing human enterprises.

Now clearly humankind has a long way to go before women are "allowed" (by men) to have much say in how things are done. One task of the 21st century is to take necessary steps to lift women out of the bondage and subjugation under which they labor all over the planet. As a father and step-father of four girls, I am grateful that they have grown up in America, where at least women are not subject to the more gross forms of suppression which drag women down all over the planet. It is also clear that even in the good old US of A, women do not receive equal pay for equal work; they rarely sit on corporate boards or occupy executive leadership roles in representative numbers; they currently have 9 of 100 seats in the U.S. Senate, 2 of 9 on the Supreme Court, and so on.

Women have, in fact, made some progress in America; nevertheless, the values of economic greed, a perpetual war-time economy, the treatment of the earth's resources as expendable for immediate profits and to hell with posterity—these are still male dictated and male implemented values. We have a long way to go to introduce the feminine principle of respect for life in all of its forms into the body politic and the national agenda.

Meanwhile, across the globe, women continue to battle for basic rights: the right to control their own economic destiny; the right to live their lives without male-imposed sexual mutilation (as in clitoridectomies); the right to education—in some countries, girls are not even allowed to go to school; the right to *not* be beaten by husbands (i.e., in Brazil, 80% of murders of women and 70% of rapes are reportedly committed by the victims' husbands, relatives, or friends); the right of young girls to not be sold into prostitution or pornography or sexual slavery (for example, "Prostitution among the children who live and work on the streets of Latin America is now estimated at up to 40 million..." *International Herald*, January 4, 2000); the right to not be one of several wives indentured to one husband; the right to receive basic education in matters of sexual importance; the right to appear in public without hiding one's face; and the list goes on. It doesn't take a Rhodes scholar to see that the common denominator of these abuses of women is men.

The terms of the struggle are clear: it is women struggling for equity, dignity, and independence in every respect against the desire of men to dominate and control their every behavior. Looked at this way, it isn't a pretty picture, and it makes one ashamed to be associated with the whole male-dominance conspiracy.

Things are changing gradually. However, the changes in parts of the world are heartbreakingly slow. The waste of talents and even lives of women in so many places is of immense proportions. So let's turn back for a moment to the Marquez idea. Most people's immediate response will be that this is a quaint idea, but one which has about as much chance as a feather in a whirlwind. Quaint, but hopelessly idealistic. Probably so. And perhaps it would be no more desirable to see the opposite sex totally dominant than to continue with the current male dominance, through it is hard to imagine women doing worse than men have done in ruling. Ultimately, the ideal would be a balance of the masculine and feminine, an equity of power, influence and opportunity. At present, we are a long way off from such harmony. While it is unlikely that most men will give more than lip service to this ideal, it is worth working towards, for all our sakes.

It seems fair to ask men to try as hard to discover or recover their feminine side, as men have required women to do in developing their masculine side in just about every arena of Western society. The human race can only benefit if a more harmonious balance is achieved within each individual as well as in society.

Paul F. Cummins

APOLOGY OVERDUE

Apologies are generally a good place to begin healing processes. Apologies imply recognition of previous or current transgressions, and that recognition may be a deterrent to future transgressions. Perhaps Pope John Paul II's recent apologies will serve such a function. At least for the Catholic Church that possibility is now stronger. I would like to see a similar international apology issued by the United States to the people of Vietnam, as well as to the U.S. soldiers who were sent there to die, to suffer lifelong wounds, and to inflict suffering on others in a war of United States aggression.

Recently, I read through a catalog of videos and came across a series on Vietnam: the advertisements made the war sound glorious and presented our soldiers as the only heroes of the war. Well, yes, the U.S. soldiers were remarkably brave in a losing cause, a cause they were forced to support. This video series, however, and many others, presents the war as either an example of powerful new technologies, or a place where Americans were hampered by political constraints (i.e., the army wasn't allowed to drop hydrogen bombs), or where the South Vietnamese people betrayed their would-be American saviors. Even Robert McNamara now admits the whole episode was pretty much a mistake, but he stops short of apologizing to the Vietnamese and stops short of taking full responsibility for his own distorted logic. He was, after all, being touted during the war years as one of our best and the brightest.

We properly lament the 56,000 American soldiers who lost their lives in this tragic war; yet we have not seen fit to lament the 3,000,000 Vietnamese–including innocent peasants, women and children–who fell victims to our carpet bombing. (More bombs were dropped on the tiny nation than we dropped in WWII.) All of this occurred because we could not tolerate the unification of Vietnam under a democratically-elected communist government.

We conveniently forget that in 1954, Vietnam was poised on the moment of independence for the first time since France had invaded it in 1847 and imposed its colonial rule. We forget that the United States became an independent nation after waging a war of revolution against British colonialism. We forget that the United States subverted the Geneva Conference in 1954, which sanctioned a national election in Vietnam, an election that Ho Chi Minh may well have won. And we forget that we joined with the French and British in preventing the reunification of Vietnam. Ironically, the subsequent Vietnam tragedy was, in part, our own creation. We now know that the domino theory was flawed, and we know that the incredible misery and devastation wreaked upon Vietnam–spilling over as well into Laos and Cambodia–were the result of American arrogance and ignorance.

It seems to me that in issuing a blanket apology to the people of Vietnam, and to the world, we might also specifically apologize for dropping chemical defoliants–*for ten years*–upon 10% of the land area that was then South Vietnam. These defoliants mainly consisted of the herbicide named Agent Orange. Today, twenty-five years later, Vietnamese, as well as American soldiers, continue to suffer from the remaining toxins in the water, the land, and in human bodies. Yet our government still maintains it needs to do more research before acknowledging responsibility. Can we pretend that saturating another country's land with poison was justified? We are appalled when we read of Suddam Hussein's chemical war waged against the Kurds. Yet somehow we can convince ourselves that it was okay for us to do the same in Vietnam. As part of the healing process, it is time to acknowledge our collective-national sins in contaminating generations of children born and (possible, in as yet unborn) by our hubris and might-makes-right arrogance of the past.

In 1971 I watched a documentary of the Vietnam veterans march on Washington D.C., during which dozens of American soldiers walked up to a microphone, and one after another held up the various medals they had won and recited their accolades–the Purple Heart, the Bronze Star, the Silver Star, the Distinguished Flying Cross, and more, and then, one after the other, threw them in a waste bin as their protest to the folly and evils of the war we were waging. I remember one soldier in particular who limped up to the podium, cited his various medals, and then proclaimed: "I'd like to say just one thing to the people of Vietnam: `God, I'm sorry!" Isn't it time for our country to follow the example set by that brave soldier almost 30 years ago?

Paul F. Cummins

PRISONS AND PROSPERITY

A confession: I am an inveterate clipper of newspaper pieces. I have files and files of them which I often refer to in writing articles. Last weekend, I was sorting out a pile when I came across two that were back-to-back, and I was startled by the juxtaposition of the articles' two headlines:

"GIDDY PROSPERITY IN AMERICA, AND NO END IN SIGHT"
"U.S. PRISON POPULATION HITS THE 2 MILLION MARK"

As a popular saying goes these days—what's wrong with this picture? Well, the first thing to acknowledge is that both headlines are accurate. Thus, what's wrong with the picture is that the world's most affluent nation is also the country with the world's most incarcerations. Yes, more than China, more than Russia, more than Columbia, you name it. We are the world's lock-'em-up leader.

Now, some may say that the juxtaposition of headlines that I found startling is really nothing to be disturbed about. In fact, I have even heard people argue that it is because we have so many "bad guys" in prison that we are able to achieve such prosperity. They argue that we "good folks" can pursue our quest for wealth unimpeded by those in jail. This is an appalling line of reasoning as well as a lump-headed one. "Appalling" because it implies that somehow two million "bad" folks were just born bad. The correlation of poverty to imprisonment doesn't seem to matter to the lump heads.

However, beyond this are a few other points: One, we are not a safe nation, i.e., we are the homicide capital of the industrial world; two, the people we put in prison often come out of prison even more chilled, mean, and hardened; three, our assumption of "bad folks, in prison—good folks, not in prison" omits the burgeoning population of white collar criminals who merely receive fines or procure expensive acquittals and do not serve time; four, many of the "bad" people we put in prisons are minority drug users who consume low-grade drugs (the wealthy cocaine-snorting folks in upper class neighborhoods are not always persecuted/ prosecuted for their habits).

In fact, as we look at who winds up in prison, it becomes more and more clear that money, class, and race determine who goes and who does not. One is hard put to avoid the conclusion that the world's most hedonistic, materialistic, consumer-mad society is also becoming one of the world's most mean-spirited nations. Not only is the discrepancy between the rich and poor widening at obscene rates, but, as Vincent Schiraldi, executive director of the Washington D.C. Justice Policy Institute, recently states, "This (the 1990's) was the most punishing decade on record." The prison population was one million in 1990 and two million in 2000. It doubled. It had taken 90 years to double prior to 1990!

So, what's going on? I offer a second confession: I don't really know. A couple of facts are clear, yet it's unclear if they tell the whole story. One theory is hard to avoid: the prison growth is a blatantly racist phenomenon. Blacks are nearly seven times more likely to be put in prison than whites. Blacks, for example, comprise about 13% of the U.S. population, yet they account for 50% of the state and federal prison population. Many of the offenses are drug-related and, while whites account for about 75% of the nation's drug users, blacks account for about 75% of the nation's drug prisoners.

Still as we put more and more people in jail for drugs, and for longer sentences, no one believes the drug war is being won. So perhaps we could spend the $40 billion dollars of taxpayer funds more expeditiously. For example, we could build more and better schools, libraries, and recreation centers to focus upon prevention rather than punishment. In too many states the inflated prison budgets undermine efforts to improve schools. Clearly, things are amiss.

In addition to racism as one explanation of what's amiss, I fear there may be another explanation—that is, the "prison-industrial complex" has become a major economic force and its own momentum is now pushing this whole incarceration frenzy. While the nation doubled its prison population in the 90s, a group of people made a boatload of money. While I don't fully know what's driving the mean-spirited profusion of prisons, I seem to detect the stench of racism and greed. And, as usual, it is the poor and minorities who are the victims. What to do? Well, let's begin by acknowledging that what we are doing is immoral, unfair, and, ultimately, unproductive. That's a good place to start.

Paul F. Cummins

ABSOLUTE TRUTH

It's difficult, isn't it, to reach a final conviction about most things? New facts, new research, new theories come along and one's favorite opinions are wrenched away and, god forbid, we often have to say, "Whoops, I was wrong about that one." I remember in high school worshipping Douglas McArthur after writing a term paper on his career. At the time, I reviled Truman for firing this great general. Later, I came to see that Douglas McArthur (referred to by William Manchester as "American Caesar") was a bit of an egomaniac, a not always so brilliant military strategist, and a myopic army man who often missed the larger picture. In retrospect, I came to see that my high school term paper was based on some rather faulty assumptions.

My next hero, the subject of a college term paper, was Woodrow Wilson. I pretty much bought the conventional story: Wilson was an idealist with a vision of world peace and a great dream of a league of nations which the Republican senators scuttled. Betrayed by his own government! Alas. But later, after more research and reading, I was forced to conclude that my college term paper substantially over-simplified the Wilson saga. Wilson, like McArthur, was another ego-driven man, incapable of compromise, and ultimately, self-destructive—not only of his own physical being, but of his dreams of world peace.

Then there was/is Teddy Roosevelt, the subject of a great deal of American folk lore and hero-worship. Teddy the Rough Rider, the man speaking from the bully pulpit, the outdoorsman, the man with the big toothy grin, the man who carried the big stick. I wrote a paper on him in college too—praising his manly, American virtues. Yet it turns out that Teddy was an imperialist of the first order, a man who confused America's supposed destiny with God's will, a man who, as William Pfaff wrote recently, "simply liked war." Another term paper slips into the disavowal file.

I am forced to wonder, what do I fervently believe today that I may find untenable tomorrow? The answer, I suppose, is I don't fully know. What I believe today, I believe because it makes the most sense today. Yet, I do not believe that everything is relative to time and place. I believe there is such a thing as logic and truth. For example, I will never be convinced that guns are anything other than an abomination; that having 200,000,000 guns on the street makes us a safer nation, or that possessing them ought to be a civil right. What *ought* to be is their complete abolition. I also believe that there ought to be a better system of the distribution of the world's opportunities, resources, and wealth; that fairness and equity are higher values than self-aggrandizement and greed. No, I don't think there is any research or new theory that will convince me that inequity is a good thing.

Nevertheless, some issues are distinctly complex. For example, while I think war is the reflection of humanity at its worst, and now recognize that the Vietnam War was a mistake, as well as an immoral undertaking, it is still unclear whether the Vietnamese people would have been better off had the United States not intervened. The conventional liberal line to which I have subscribed for over twenty years, is that if we had kept our nose out of Vietnam, then Ho Chi Minh would have won the 1954 elections, would have unified the country under communist rule, and some two million Vietnamese people would have been spared their lives. And certainly this is one possible scenario. However, a Vietnamese friend recently offered a different argument. He claims that Ho was a butcher who killed thousands of his own Vietnamese people when the north invaded the south; he reports that ever since 1975, communist rule has been intolerable for many Vietnamese people who have lost their land, jobs, and liberty, and that the American's presence was welcomed by many south Vietnamese who were rightly terrified of a communist regime.

Is there a correct view? Probably there is not one simple explanation, no one truth. I am convinced that the Vietnamese people would have been better off without "the American war," as they refer to the 1961-1975 tragedy. Two million Vietnamese dead is a heavy price to pay for trying to influence someone else's politics. Nevertheless, it is a complicated picture.

Where does this all lead? What conclusions do I draw from having to revise former opinions and historical views? Only this: That history is ambiguous at best, and human beings are a bundle of conflicting desires and values and, therefore, that nothing is as simple as we all, ideologues on the right or the left, proclaim. Having said that, I would add that there are some immutable truths–whether my detractors agree or not. If they don't agree, then they are just flatly wrong. Inequity and poverty are an abomination. Guns are a manifestation of humanity at its worst, slaughtering animals and eliminating hundreds of species per day is a sin against the future, and befouling the land, air, and seas for quick profits at the expense of all tomorrows and for all future generations is absolutely wrong. We can debate the merits of Douglas McArthur or the American intervention in Vietnam, but some things are not debatable. There are some values which require our adherence if we are to remain truly human. As C.S. Lewis wrote in his brilliant and still immensely relevant 1947 study, The Abolition of Man, there are some judgments that, "are not mere sentiments, but are rationality itself." Finding those correct judgments is our impossible yet challenging task as parents, teachers, and citizens of the globe.

Paul F. Cummins

TO WHOM MUCH IS GIVEN

In the three presidential debates of the 2000 election, Gov. G.W. Bush stated several times that his primary motive for foreign policy would be "what's best for American interests." He spoke of only in terms of military action, and there, he said, "The object is to win wars." He did not, however, suggest the possibility of a more noble and humanitarian goal of our foreign policy–to help those in dire, life and death need of help. Nor, for that matter, did the opponent Al Gore have much to say about such a goal.

Back in 1936, in his inaugural address, FDR said, "For those to whom much is given, much is expected." I'm afraid this notion has been pretty much lost in our economic boom times which has encouraged a new round of frenzied greed for quick profits. While we Americans out-consume the rest of the world by a piggish margin, somewhere between 15,000 to 20,000 children around the world die each day of starvation. While we use the world's resources at a disproportionate rate and disproportionately add to the world's garbage, waste, and toxic problems, much of the rest of the world struggles to eke out some kind of existence. Not only is it unfair, it is unnecessary.

How so, you may ask? Because if we shifted our attitudes from asking, as the President wants to ask, "What's in America's best interests?" and asked instead, "What's in the best interests of children all over the world?" then a whole new set of objectives opens up.

For example, the President argues that our military is weak, that we must keep the military-industrial budget at its higher-than-cold-war level and, therefore, enable the corporate giants of industry (who support both Gore and Bush) to keep amassing their obscene profits unabated. However, as William Greider, in his 1997 study, *Fortress America*, points out, not only is the Pentagon sitting on huge surpluses of airplanes and armored vehicles, they and their industrial suppliers are frantically seeking foreign countries to purchase our weapons and airplanes and the like. If we are so worried about our military being prepared, why then are we arming the rest of the world? As Greider further points out: "They [the military-industrial folks] aren't making the world safer. By pushing more and more weaponry, old and new, on other nations, the arms manufacturers are laying the groundwork for future conflicts."

Is our military unprepared or are our values distorted? If, however, we chose to shift some of our ludicrous **over**-spending on military preparedness for non-existent or weak enemies into supporting the economies and education of under-developed nations, then several things would occur: One, we might make more friends rather than engendering the envious hatred that we now experience all over the globe; two, by helping other nations become better educated and more self-sufficient, we might actually make the world a safer place for **our** children; and three, by helping others to have viable economies, we can help slow down the degradation of the global environment. For example, a nation not wholly dependent on timber will not need to destroy the rain forests of the world–which, in turn, diminishes **all** our futures.

The presidential debates, sadly, did not include any awareness of what the average eighth grade student (at schools that I co-founded, Crossroads and New Roads, and schools across the country) are expected to understand: That the ecology of the earth and all its life, human and otherwise, are interdependent. Perhaps the low level of voter turn-out and citizen participation is a reflection not of voter apathy, but of disgust with our leaders, and with the media.

In any event, I believe the challenge of the younger generation is to go way beyond the "America first" mentality that is often peddled in politics and to see that putting the delicate interconnected tissue of the world's needs as our highest priority is ultimately, albeit ironically what is in America's best interests. I believe that, increasingly, young people are coming to this realization. This is what gives me hope. I just wish there were a few world leaders, especially American politicians, who had the courage to see and speak this truth and to act upon it.

Paul F. Cummins

SOUR GRAPES

I confess I am depressed, discouraged, demoralized, and, to a degree, bitter. Excellence isn't a common commodity. By its very nature, it is uncommon. However, in a nation of 250 million people, surely there are qualified women and men who possess the kind of excellence of mind and spirit that the chief executive officer of the land should possess. Instead, our country elects to be its president a Richard Nixon, and a Ronald Reagan, and a George Bush Sr., and now a Jr. None of them has shown an ability to write with distinction. Only one even read books (Mr. Nixon). So far as I can tell, none of them have had anything resembling an original thought. None of them belongs in the same league with a Thomas Jefferson, or an Abraham Lincoln, or a Woodrow Wilson. I believe what we see in the four presidents: Nixon, Reagan, Sr. Bush and Jr. represent the dumbing down of American politics.

I realize that all four are Republicans and that my views, therefore, appear highly partisan, but consider a few contrasts. Jimmy Carter is clearly a literate, well-read, articulate man. Bill Clinton, leaving aside his peccadillos, is a voracious reader and student of economics. I believe, however, that we have had twelve-years (1980-1992) when the United States President did not read one book! We know pretty much that Reagan didn't (though he did watch over 350 movie re-runs at Camp David during his terms). And, there is no evidence that Bush read anything other than briefings. And George W., a mediocre student once, is perhaps the least articulate president we have elected in over 100 years. During one of the debates, "W" even made a joke about his "mangling" of the English language and, of course, the American public found it endearing. But I was, and am, appalled that the President and leader of the free world can't handle his own native language with any skill and finds his inability laughable.

Perhaps the American public doesn't think it matters that the president be bright, be an original thinker, and/or be an intellect of any kind. In fact, we are told American males didn't like Al Gore because he appeared to be a know-it-all as opposed to W. who appeared to know very little. But it matters to me, and that's why I'm depressed and bitter.

I used to think that God was punishing me personally for my sins by inflicting Richard Nixon upon me for so many years–in California, then in the White House. Why, I wondered, couldn't I have a president to admire, a president with a first-rate mind and an enlightened view of the globe and its problems and possibilities? Then I was further punished by eight years of a script-reader and four years of a man who used verbs without subjects. And now W. When will it end?

Is it not possible to elect a president who is more than just a good old boy, not just one whom the average or below-average American male likes because he or she doesn't appear to be too smart? Isn't it possible that we might elect someone because he or she is brilliant in addition to being politically adept? Isn't it possible to elect a college graduate who did more than drink, snort, and be a good frat boy, but instead who plunged deeply into subjects, wrote distinguished papers and theses, and actually exhibited a passion for learning?

I thought JFK fit the mold, but I'm not sure now that he was as much substance as style, though we'll never know what he might have become. Clinton was not only a Rhodes scholar, but a real student of global economics. His personal life, however, impeded his effectiveness. But, dear readers, G.W.B.? What have we done to ourselves? I don't know what's worse, the actual mediocrity of the man, or that people want and can only relate to mediocrity, or that the public doesn't even know what mediocrity is any more, such being our over-all, dumbed-down condition. Or is it equally distasteful that intelligent people could want a mediocre president who will leave them alone in their pursuit of unbridled economic gain?

But none of the options portend well for our nation. I expect W. to allow more environmental de-regulation, find a few more Scalias and Clarence Thomases, appease the far right (who behaved as they were seemingly instructed to do and shut up for the six months preceding the election), and basically let corporate America continue to run the show.

Yeah, I'm bitter and demoralized. Just once in my adult life I'd like to have a president I could really respect, admire, and look ***up*** to.

Paul F. Cummins

THE COURAGE TO BE

When the democratic presidential candidate–in the heat of a national election–loses 3-5% overnight in a national poll because he sighed on TV, when the vice president of eight years in the midst of a booming economy fails to trounce his inexperienced opponent, when a large percentage of the voters are "undecided" a week before the election, and when half of the registered voters, the majority of whom are Democrats, don't vote, you have to wonder if the Democratic Party has lost its way. Clearly the voters in the 2000 election saw little difference between the two parties. Moving to the center, while averting a temporary Gingrich coup, probably has not served the party well for the long run.

I, therefore, suggest a not-so-new, not-so-startling, but perhaps critical proposition for the party: return to your Roosevelt (FDR) roots, distinguish yourself from the Republicans, give the middle class, lower-middle class, lower class, disenfranchised, economically struggling and deprived peoples a reason to come to the polls. Return to a more populist position. Bring the Nader-green-social justice advocates back into the fold.

How to go about this? Well, for one thing, articulate clearly and forcefully the real differences between the parties. They exist. During the 2000 campaign, Vice President Gore was so afraid (so ill-advised) of appearing "too liberal" that he did not make clear the very important distinctions between the two parties. One, Democrats favor increasing the minimum wages–Republicans oppose it. Two, Democrats favor protecting our rapidly diminishing and degraded environmental resources; Republicans see the environment primarily as economic resources for quick profits and not as the beautiful heritage of both current and future generations. Three, Democrats favor expanding the rights of women and minorities; Republicans offer lip-service but oppose virtually every specific bill aimed at expanding those rights. Al Gore failed to draw such distinctions. Consequently, voters who should have passionately and eagerly sought to vote, stayed home. They simply did not believe he or the party represented their interests.

I believe Al Gore won the election–not just the popular vote but Florida as well. It never should have come down to the other Governor Bush's state to decide the contest. In part, Ralph Nader cost Gore Florida–along with all the irregularities in Florida–but it was clear at the end that many Nader supporters were teetering and even changing their minds. Gore simply didn't give them enough reasons or any inspiration to vote for him. Gore, the author of Earth in the Balance, couldn't make one unequivocal statement showing his passion for environmental defense. He had to temper his few comments about ecology with obeisance to the economy–a code message to corporations that he would not really hurt their efforts at continuing to exploit the environment for profits today! Now, while this may have reassured some corporate supporters, it did little to encourage any Democratic Party members who care about the environment to abandon Nader and vote for Gore.

I believe those who advised Vice President Gore to stay the middle of the road course served him poorly. The Democratic Party needs to find within itself the courage to say what it believes that is *different* from what Republicans believe. Potential voters need a reason to vote. It won't do to say "we are just like the other guys." If that is so, then why vote? It makes no difference. It is the differences that makes people want to vote. This last election degenerated into a sort of pathetic popularity contest: who sighed, who seemed more sincere, who seemed to be a know-it-all. None of these has anything to do with ideas, issues, policies. But if the ideas, issues, and policies seem the same, then voters are left with the candidate with the more winning smile. I hope the Democratic leadership will see this past election as a clarion call–for the courage to be what the party at its best used to be and needs to become again.

Paul F. Cummins

THE LOONY BIN OR THE PEN?

What do you do when your ideas seem completely at odds with the prevailing canons? One option is to commit yourself to an institution for the deranged. Another is to leave your current environment and find a place where your views are in harmony with the majority. Another, and the option I have chosen, is to simply state your views publicly in hopes that they will have an impact and will seem more compelling. As the new administration in Washington pushes its agenda of tax cuts for the rich, I can only reiterate my own minority view that calls for just the opposite: increased taxation and increased spending to redress societal injustices, to rebuild our nation's infrastructure, to clean up the mess in education, and to preserve what's left of our rapidly disappearing and compromised environment.

I observe the current groundswell of sentiment–or at least the media's obedient proclaiming of such a groundswell–for tax cuts, and I am flabbergasted. If we have a surplus, the argument of the power-structure runs, we should return it to "the people." The people, who benefit most, of course, turn out to be (in the George "Dubya" plan) already wealthy people. "They made most of it, they should get most of it back," say the GWB forces.

Now, GWB, et.al., never acknowledge that "they who made it" did so with the help of an enormous corporate welfare support system. The GWB team would have us believe that somehow "they" made their enormous profits in a societal vacuum with only their individualistic, entrepreneurial initiative to support them. Never mind the huge tax breaks they have received from the government since the "Reagan Revolution," never mind the government services, subsidies, enabling laws and legislation and de-regulation and anti-anti-trust policies. No, "they" did it all on their own and "they" should, therefore, not only get the bulk of the surplus back, "they" should get an honorific bonus of further tax cuts.

Meanwhile, the gap between CEO's and workers continues to widen: from 42-to-1 in 1980 to 419-to-1 in 2000. The number of children living in poverty in the United States is somewhere around one in five; in addition, 16.5% of all Americans live in poverty, even though the United States leads the world in per-capita consumption of good and services. Consider also that the richest 20% of Americans earn 8.9 times more than the poorest 20%. This is on a par with the rich/poor gap in Kenya and about twice as bad as that in Bangladesh and Rwanda.

Never mind these issues; let's give the wealthy more help and to hell with the poor children, to hell with the inner-city schools, to hell with the low income workers, and to hell with the rivers, oceans, soil, trees, and the very atmosphere itself. "They who made it big need more." And now "they" have the backing of Bretheren in Washington to accomplish their goal, to get the most benefits they so richly deserve. An oil president, an oil vice president, a secretary of the interior who favors business over ecology, and various other foxes to guard the chicken coops. It is truly a depressing scenario and it has just begun. The next four years have only just begun.

So what are outsiders like me, and perhaps a few readers, to do? Well, there is always the opportunity to squawk a little. Those of us who oppose the prevailing winds at least have a few places to express our opposition views. Since I'm not completely loony, the option of committing myself to an institution doesn't seem appropriate. And since I do love my country (though not when it's wrong), I don't want to live anywhere else. Thus, option three, speaking out, is all that remains.

My alternative suggestions: 1) we should put our current surplus into social and educational amelioration plans; 2) we should *not* cut taxes; 3) we should actually *increase* sales taxes on harmful products such as guns, ammunition, cigarettes, and gasoline; 4) we should *cut* defense spending and *increase* spending on poor children, libraries, the arts, and protecting our land and natural resources; and, 5) under no circumstances should we put funds into the idiotic "star wars" boondoggle. I know that "star wars" is a sweet gift to the military-industrial-techno-corporate folks, but it is a misguided and unnecessary mis-spending of funds desperately needed elsewhere.

So, with little hope of any concurrence from the folks in Washington, or from the general media, I will continue to offer minority opinions and hope that my words reach a few kindred souls out there who will nod in agreement and appreciation.

Paul F. Cummins

THE REAL QUESTION/THE REAL ANSWER

Here we go again–and again, and again. A handgun massacre of students. This time, again, by a student who never should have had a gun. Again, the television and newspaper images of sobbing parents and friends–their lives forever ruined. Again, there will be articles, panels, study groups, and the questions will reoccur: How could a boy like Charles Andrew Williams have done what he did? "He didn't seem like the type." "He was only 15 years old." "He got picked on, but not so much more than any other teenager in a world where adolescent cruelty is the norm."

The New York Times has already devoted long articles to examining how this could happen, *but nowhere is the real question asked, or the real solution posed*. But I'll come back to that.

Meanwhile, the discussion groups will proliferate. How can we reach out more to disturbed kids like Charles Andrew? How can we see tragedies like this coming sooner? How can we make our campuses more safe? How can we design more appropriate courses, programs, activities to encourage students to become engaged in positive activities? [Or, as the Los Angeles Times asked, "How can we tell which teen will kill?"] All good questions, *but not the real question and not the real solution*. But I'll get to that shortly.

And, as the weeks pass, the students of Santana High School and the citizens of Santee, California will provide funerals, ceremonies honoring their deep losses, assemblies to provide support and solace for each other. The rest of the country will be momentarily sad, perhaps relieved it didn't happen in their neighborhood, yet having a foreboding sense that it just as easily could have and may yet occur. And then, Santee will join the list of tragic handgun massacres of our young including Columbine High School in Littleton, and now Santee. We will all go back to our day-to-day lives, and *the real questions will not be posed, and the real solution will be ignored*. But I will get to that soon.

The government will, perhaps, be compelled to do some further tinkering with gun control. A safety latch here, another day's registration wait there before buying a gun. The latest goal is to design guns that only the owner can use. This should help victim's families feel better, knowing that <u>their</u> loved ones were shot by the actual owner of the gun. However, in the end, the government will do little and will certainly not ask *the real question or pose the real solution*.

Why will the real question and real solution <u>**not**</u> be seriously considered? Why is America the handgun homicide capital of the planet? Why are there over 250,000,000 handguns out on the streets? Why do citizens think owning guns makes us safe when it so clearly, patently, blatantly makes us the most dangerous nation in the world? Does not Santee remind us that our children are not even safe at school because of the epidemic flood of guns in our society?

The answer to these questions **is** clear. We love our guns. Bumper stickers proudly proclaim: "I love my Smith and Wesson." Whether gun possession assuages our deep seated fears of masculinity (let's face it—it is mostly men who love guns), or whatever the psycho-socio-logical explanation, we dearly love our guns and would rather continue to endure Columbines, Santees, and 10,000-15,000 other gun homicides per year (compared to 50 or so in England and Japan) than to ask *the real question and offer real solutions*.

We also hide behind the Constitution. It's our Constitutional right to bear arms, argues the NRA, the right wing, and other old-fashioned, red-blooded Americans. The Second Amendment states, in whole: "A well-regulated Militia being necessary to the security of a Free State, the right of the people to keep and bear arms shall not be infringed." As I interpret this, it is the militia that needs the arms, and since we now have an army, and the army can keep its own weapons on its own sites, we don't need individual citizens to store guns as if they were the militia. Let's wake up—neither the "Red Coats" nor the "Reds" are coming. The enemy is *us*, and the thousands of us **we** kill every year.

The real question is: *Why do we have more guns on the street than any other country in the world?* And the real answer is: *There is no good reason. Abolish them!*

Paul F. Cummins

EVIL OR IGNORANCE?

I suppose George W. Bush and his corporate cronies and congressional cohorts have ways of convincing themselves that selling out the environment to economic interests is good. I mean that they feel they are good people doing good things for the greater good of us all. I suppose that they go to sleep each night with a sense that they are honorable people upholding high ideals. I suppose that they believe they are protecting America from a lunatic fringe who are needlessly alarmist and pessimistic about the supposed degradation of the environment.

I have to suppose these things; otherwise, it would be even more depressing than it is, watching the corporate power structure continue to destroy the most beautiful and precious living organism–Earth–in the known universe. For if the Bush-corporate partnership did not believe as I have supposed, they would either be ignorant, lunatics, or evil. For the reality is–by scientific incontrovertible measurements–that we, the human-techno-profiteering-race, are destroying our own planet's life cycles at a dramatic and probably even irreversible rate. And while this goes on, the Bush-corporate conglomerate acts as if it is moral and prudent to ignore all visible and verifiable evidence to the contrary. In fact, President Bush's actions in his first few months of office were stunning beyond comprehension (except that we could only expect such behavior from a Texas-corpo-oilman). While environmental groups all over the world are calling on Mr. Bush to bring the United States back to the climate talks (which the United States recently torpedoed at the Hague), and to take urgent action to reduce United States carbon dioxide emissions, what does our President do? He disowns a campaign pledge and says his administration will not seek to regulate power plants' emissions of carbon dioxide, a gas which is a key contributor to global warming.

So, we return to my initial premise: he must believe these actions are moral, but how, I wonder in utter disbelief, can he? United States greenhouse gas emissions rose nearly 12% in the 1990s according to a recent EPA report (www.epa.gov/globalwarming/ publications/emissions). "American cars, factories, and power plants emit 25 percent of the heat trapping gases in the atmosphere, making the U.S. the world's biggest producer of greenhouse gases." (Rachel Rivers, The Amicus Journal, Spring 2001) And, according to the latest report from the U.N. Intergovernmental Panel on Climate Change, the planet is warming even faster than experts have predicted.

In the face of this threat to the future of the entire planet, our president and we who sit by and tacitly approve, are concerned with helping our corporations profit just a little bit more. It is so short sighted as to truly beggar the imagination and the intellect.

Daily we add to the list of species becoming extinct, and daily we reduce the amount of trees, fish in the ocean, animals on the Earth, arable soil, water we can drink and our leaders are only mindful of American corporations' needs to make maximum profits. The latest proposal is to open the Arctic National Wildlife Refuge–one of the world's last pristine wild places–to oil (surprise!) development. Mr. Bush argues this would lessen United States dependence on foreign fuel and also lower gasoline prices. In fact, oil from the Arctic Refuge would contribute less than 1% of U.S. oil needs over the next fifty years. But, of course, sinking oil wells would do lasting damage to the flora and fauna of the region. Once again, the new administration shows its priorities: profits over posterity.

Which leads me back to my original puzzlement. Have these heads of state really convinced themselves that their behavior is in *our*–the citizens and our descendants–best interests? Can they really believe that the quick profits of a segment of one generation supersede the rights of generations to come to enjoy the beauty and rapidly diminishing variety of the natural world? Is this their sadly deluded system of belief? Or are they simply greedy profiteers hiding behind "compassionate" consumerist rhetoric? Either way, we are all the losers.

Paul F. Cummins

WHERE HAVE ALL THE FROGGIES GONE?

I have some startling news for the Bush administration, which I am certain they will want to immediately attend to with all the might of their power and wisdom. The news is this: frogs, salamanders and their kin are disappearing all over the world. Recently, a global estimate conducted by an international team found a decline of 60 to 70 percent in the species for the past few decades! "Some areas have suffered even more severely and 20 species are presumed extinct." (*The Chronicle of Higher Education*, April 20, 2001). Now, while I am certain this news will spur Mr. Bush and Mr. Cheney into immediate action, just in case others in his administration are not concerned, I offer the following concerns not only of mine, but of scientists all over the world. (For those citizens and the Bush administration folks interested in further explanation, I suggest reading The Worldwatch Institute's annual book, *State of the World 2001*.)

The sudden decline of amphibians all over the world is of concern for a variety of reasons. One, these creatures have been in existence for over 350 million years and have survived three mass extinctions. Yet, in a historic wink, they are disappearing. Two, these creatures are part of our ancestry. They were the first vertebrates to evolve from water to land, and after them came other vertebrates–reptiles, birds, mammals, and us! And, according to Ashley Mattoon, in her Worldwatch article "Deciphering Amphibian Declines," she writes: "Given their durability and ubiquity, the rapid decline of so many species is particularly unsettling... Many scientists claim that amphibians are important bio-indicators–a sort of barometer of Earth's health." And this is, of course, the major issue. It isn't just frogs that are disappearing. The frogs' disappearance is a manifestation of environmental degradation in general, and the health of all living creatures is inextricably intertwined. But back to frogs for a few moments.

What are the causes of the rapid disappearance of frogs? Scientists have some but not all the answers. There are, however, a few clear factors. One, and the leading cause, is habitat loss. According to Professor Rick A. Reyala, a biologist at the University of Pittsburgh, "It [habitat loss] is the dominant factor in the declines of most animals–that we are taking their habitat away." How? By urban sprawl, by clear-cutting and logging and other deforestation measures, by eliminating rain forests and wet lands and streambeds, by conversion of grasslands to farms and suburban developments–the whole sorry list. The major culprit in all this habitat loss is us–homo sapiens. So, theoretically, we could, if we wake up in time, reverse some of the damage we have done, are doing, and–if not addressed–will continue to do.

The second major cause is the use of toxic pesticides in their various forms. Study after study shows that this is so even in seemingly pristine areas where no humans are present. But, alas, *our* pesticides are brought in by the wind, by streams and underground watersheds. According to Richard Monastersky, "This scenario seems to be playing out in the Sierra Nevada mountains of California where frog populations have declined precipitously even in national parks." (*The Chronicle of Higher Education*, April 20, 2001)

A third cause is climate change. And here, Mr. Bush, we have some real ***hard science*** where experiments have shown that global warming "has exerted a subtle but profound effect–killing off toads [in Oregon] there through a complex series of changes." (Richard Monastersky)

A fourth cause is the human introduction of non-native species into certain areas where they then feed upon the amphibians causing further disruption to the ecological balance.

So, why should we care about frogs? Because, as I said earlier, they are literally our ancestors, because they are beautiful and interesting, because they are living, complex chemical factories, and their loss "could also mean the loss of potential cures for many common [human] ailments" (Ashley Mattoon), because they are sensitive creatures that may well be "canaries in a coal mine" showing us impending problems for all species including our own, and, finally, because they share this earth with us and are an important part of the ecological chain–that's why.

I know this news will not come as a surprise to Mr. Bush–a notoriously sensitive environmentalist–but I hope he will enlighten his administration colleagues so that they will jump right on this problem. But, in case it slips his mind, perhaps you too, gentle reader, will spread the word of our alarming loss of frogs. Killing off our frog population spells equally serious trouble for all of us who live on this planet. In short, every environmental problem the frogs face confronts us as well. We are *all* in this together. A planet with sick and dying frogs is not a healthy planet for humans.

Paul F. Cummins

WHAT'S THE DIFFERENCE?

So, what is the difference between a politician and a statesman? No, this is not a joke. It's a bona fide question. You may have your answers; here are some "classic" definitions. As you will see, the word "politician" has come to mean something less than its original positive and even laudable denotations. Its current connotations are rather unsavory. For example, here are some recent–as in the last 100 years or so–characterizations of a "politician."

Ambrose Bierce wrote, "An eel in the fundamental mud which the super-structure of organized society is reared. When he wriggles, he mistakes the agitation of his tail for the trembling of the edifice. As compared with a statesman, he suffers the disadvantage of being alive." (1906) Bierce also issued a definition of politics as "the strife of interests masquerading as a contest of principles. The conduct of public affairs for private advantage."

Then there is this comment from George Bernard Shaw: "He knows nothing; he thinks he knows everything–that clearly points to a political career."

And, of course, no set of quotes about politics would be complete without Will Rogers: "The business of government is to keep the government out of business–that is, unless business needs government aid."

And, finally, before I launch into my own commentary, a few random quotes: "What this country needs is more unemployed politicians." (Edward Langley) And "When I was a boy I was told that anybody could become president; I'm beginning to believe it." (Clarence Darrow)

Furthermore, what these and literally hundreds of other quotes attest to is the general public disillusionment with politics so pervasive today. Over half the registered voters don't bother to vote, and intelligent and enlightened young people laugh at the suggestion that they go into politics. Politics and politicians have become derogatory words.

The sadness in all of this is that we need enlightened leaders now more than ever. The degradation of our planetary eco-system, the world-wide population and concomitant economic crises, terrorism, massive poverty, world hunger and diasporas and epidemics all cry for the attention of statesmen.

A statesman by my definition is someone who embraces posterity as a higher value than quick profits and selfish interests. A statesman, for example, would favor environmental conservation over quick, profitable depletion of natural resources and beauty because a statesman would be looking beyond today to the heritage of all future citizens. A statesman would be leading the way to nuclear disarmament rather than starting a new round of arms build-ups and arms industry boondoggles. A statesman would seek ways to cooperate with the other nations of the world rather than making it clear that his nation is the one that sets all the rules. A statesman would pour every resource possible into addressing poverty and all its concomitant social evils at home rather than increasing the existing disparities of wealth and providing new tax cuts for the very wealthy.

Statesmen do not ignore the best available environmental science by saying "we don't know enough yet" and thus allowing continuing profits for those exploiting the environment. This is a greedy excuse to continue doing harm. It is what politicians do: they fatten the profits of those who bought them their election victories. Statesmen look beyond quick defense fixes that profit a few people but do not fix the deeper problems of an arms race and nuclear proliferation. Politicians do this, but statesmen do not.

As James Freeman Clarke writes, "The difference between a politician and a statesman is: A politician thinks of the next elections, and a statesman thinks of the next generation."

Paul F. Cummins

TO LIBERATE THE FUTURE FROM THE PAST

The twentieth century was, arguably, the most disastrous in human history. World wars, genocide, fratricide, global diaspora, and extinction of species at an unprecedented rate are but a few characteristics of 20th century darkness. Our past misconceptions, ideologies, and myths have largely created the ongoing horrors of history. Unless we can recognize, examine, and reverse the patterns of the past, we will continue our reckless and self-defeating behaviors in each new present moment–that is, in our future.

The chief villains reappear in century after century. They have been worse in our century because of the power which industry and technology bestowed upon them. These villains are acquisitiveness, hierarchical dominance, classism-racism-genderism, and religious fanaticism. Expressed differently, they are oligarchy, totalitarianism, patriarchy, and theocracy. Furthermore, these villains are closely, if not incestuously, related to each other. Lust for acquisition has led both to imperialism and war, as well as to a global economic system of international capitalism in which fewer oligarchs and global corporations are amassing and controlling vaster wealth. Consequently, a world-wide social system consisting of a very few rich, a modest number of moderately well-off people, and growing hordes of poor, exploited, and desperate peoples is evolving. White men are, as always, the dominant lords of the world economy. And, sadly, many religions around the world are fanatical forces maintaining the status quo and distracting serious reform by fomenting hatred of other religions and their peoples.

All in all, it is a depressing scenario, and serious reform is obstructed not only by the systems outlined above, but by the histories and myths which govern and limit our ways of looking at the world. Our histories are generally apologies for the systems which exist. They are the stories of the winners–commissioned, written, and published *by* the winners. Consequently, the losers' stories are not only not told, they are, by default, defined as unimportant and useless. Thus, the assault upon and subjugation of the poor by the rich is given justification at every level of power.

Meanwhile, a new assault is becoming ever more threatening: the assault of man upon the Earth itself. The co-myths of human progress and of man's dominion over the Earth are largely responsible for this assault. The rape and destruction of the earth are justified in the names of progress and transcendence. Capitalism-oligarchy-hierarchy–all enable the few to exploit both other peoples and the planet. Concurrently, the Judeo-Christian myth of human beings as caretakers of this earth–prior (in the Christian myth) to ascending to greater rewards in heaven–enables human beings to see themselves as transcendent to the Earth rather than being interdependent creatures "of the Earth." We have failed to see that our uniqueness lies in our having emerged from the Earth and having become conscious beings. We are thus the earth having become conscious of itself.

Nevertheless, all is not hopeless. We are "between stories"–between the old stories of winners, of progress, of transcendence, and the new stories that are emerging. Many people are coming to see just how mysterious the Earth system truly is and that somewhere within this mystery is where our salvation as a people lies. Planetary consciousness, interdependence, ecological awareness, turning inward, and questioning the status quo–all these will help bring the new stories into being.

Establishing new schools will help this process along. Schools to help students liberate their thinking from the rigid ideas of the past in order to liberate the future from prisons of the past. These new schools will offer curricula focusing upon the values of peaceful coexistence of humans with humans and of humans with nature. Finally, new schools and new visionaries must recognize, teach, and enlighten others about the necessity of designing a more equitable distribution of the world's resources and opportunities.

This new way of being and acting will birth the new stories. Clearly, some sort of world federation will be required to combat the increasing poverty and the growing global feudalism, as well as to halt the destruction and pollution of the Earth itself. We need to traverse beyond nations and united nations to become a united beings–beings to include all forms of life upon the Earth. Until now, much of modern history has been an unbroken series of patterns and assaults imposed upon the many and upon the Earth itself by the privileged few. To liberate the future from the past will require the reversal of this pattern.

ABOUT THE AUTHOR

After a long career of teaching, Paul Cummins set about to create schools–first Crossroads School in Santa Monica, California, then New Roads School in Santa Monica and Los Angeles, and then partnering with others to create a charter school–Camino Nuevo Charter Academy in Los Angeles. As of August 2001, these three schools occupy nine campuses. Often called a visionary, Cummins has combined curricular and school innovation with skills of fundraising and implementation. He also started an arts foundation that provides the arts to ten public school sites, and is currently working on a new vision of creating an inclusive and interactive educational village of various non-profits serving children. Along with all this he has written two books: ***Dachau Song: The Twentieth Century Odyssey of Herbert Zipper*** (translated also into German and Chinese) and ***For Mortal Stakes: Solutions for Schools and Society*** (translated also into Japanese), has published numerous poems, and has written ***Keeping Watch***, a compilation of articles from the *Santa Monica Mirror* newspaper, which represents a new foray into journalism and social commentary.

www.ingramcontent.com/pod-product-compliance
Lightning Source LLC
Chambersburg PA
CBHW051448280526
45785CB00003B/1481